725

Civil Liberties Under
ATTACK

Civil Liberties Under
ATTACK

By *HENRY STEELE COMMAGER*

ROBERT K. CARR · ZECHARIAH CHAFEE, Jr.

WALTER GELLHORN · CURTIS BOK

JAMES P. BAXTER, III

Essay Index Reprint Series

BOOKS FOR LIBRARIES PRESS, INC.
FREEPORT, NEW YORK

The Authors

HENRY STEELE COMMAGER · Professor of History at Columbia University; author of *The Heritage of America* and *America: the Story of a Free People.*

ROBERT K. CARR · Joel Parker Professor of Law and Political Science at Dartmouth College; Executive Secretary of the President's Committee on Civil Rights.

ZECHARIAH CHAFEE, Jr. · University Professor at Harvard University; author of *Freedom of Speech* and *Free Speech in the United States.*

WALTER GELLHORN · Professor of Law at Columbia University; author of *Security, Loyalty, and Science.*

CURTIS BOK · President Judge of the Court of Common Pleas, No. 6, Philadelphia; author of *Backbone of the Herring.*

JAMES P. BAXTER, III · President of Williams College; author of *Scientists Against Time.*

✿   ✿   ✿   ✿

CLAIR WILCOX, *Editor* · Joseph Wharton Professor of Political Economy at Swarthmore College.

Contents

Foreword

WE AMERICANS are having the jitters again. We have had them before and we have got over them. We shall doubtless survive the present attack as well. But the seizure, while it lasts, is painful. It may well drag on for years. And it is certain to leave its scar upon us.

We are afraid—afraid, for one thing, that communism will overthrow our government by resort to force and violence. But this is a fear that has no conceivable foundation in fact. Our people number more than one hundred and fifty million. The members of the Communist Party in America number a scant fifty thousand. They and all their sympathizers compose an insignificant fraction of one per cent of our population. And they are under constant surveillance. To suppose that this tiny minority could ever succeed in overwhelming our police, our army, and all of our people is to indulge in a preposterous flight of fancy.

But we are even more afraid of something else. We are afraid that communism as an idea may capture the minds and the hearts of our people. And this fear is equally groundless. Communism—save, perhaps, in China—has won its victories, not by persuasion, but by force. Its propaganda can carry conviction to the masses only where they live in ignorance and poverty, without justice and without hope. In America, of all places, it must fall upon deaf ears. Our standard of living has risen steadily over the past century; today it is the highest on earth. We have been moving toward the reduction of inequality, the removal of racial discrimination, and the assurance of social security. Our people have been free to think and to speak as they like. The doors of opportunity stand open. In our America, the conditions that could win large numbers of converts to communism simply do not exist.

And yet we are afraid. We seem to fear that communism—with its suppression of liberty, its secret police, its forced labor, and its concentration camps; with its utter denial of human dignity—would somehow win out if we were to allow it freely to compete in the market place of ideas. But surely our fear is without reason. Our society is strong enough to withstand criticism. Our citizens are intelligent enough to distinguish between black and white. To think otherwise is to confess to a loss of faith in the validity of our institutions. It is to confess to a profound distrust in the wisdom of our people.

Foolishly fearing that loyalty will not be freely given, we are now as foolishly insisting that dissent be suppressed and conformity coerced. But loyalty cannot be won in this way. And even if it could, suppression and coercion would be alien to our most cherished traditions. They are not the methods of democracy; they are the methods of totalitarianism. And when we adopt them, we pay to our enemies the ultimate flattery of imitation. We surrender our proudest possession—our essential liberties—before they have fired a single shot.

The words of Milton and Voltaire, of Thomas Jefferson and John Stuart Mill, are as true today as when they were written one, two, and three centuries ago. We have been exposed to them in our schools and colleges. But they do not seem to have taken root in our minds. When the going is easy, we take freedom for granted. When the going is hard, we permit its values to be lost from sight. In every generation, we must discover them anew.

Freedom grows in strength through exercise. If we are to preserve it, we must make use of it. We must make our voices heard whenever and wherever it is assailed. In our day, again, the time has come when those who love liberty must speak out.

The present crisis has called forth a number of notable additions to the literature of civil liberties in the United States: Alan Barth's *The Loyalty of Free Men,* Harold D. Lasswell's *National Security and Individual Freedom,* published under the auspices of the Committee for Economic Development, the *Cornell Studies in Civil Liberty,* of which Professor Gellhorn's *Security, Loyalty, and Science* is a part, and a special issue of the *Annals of the American Academy of Political and Social Science,* edited by Professor Carr. In this worthy company, the present volume of lectures, delivered at Swarthmore College on the William J. Cooper Foundation, can take a proud place. Its authors are eminent, not only as scholars, but also as champions of the great American tradition of human freedom. In the midst of nation-wide hysteria, they speak in the calm tones of common sense.

CLAIR WILCOX

Henry Steele Commager

THE PRAGMATIC NECESSITY FOR FREEDOM

$\mathcal{F}$REEDOM of speech and of the press—that is, freedom of inquiry, criticism, and dissent—are guaranteed in State and Federal Constitutions now over a century and a half old. It is a sobering fact, however, that each generation has to vindicate these freedoms anew, and for itself. Yet this is not wholly a misfortune; one might almost see in it Providential wisdom. For there are risks in taking things for granted, risks not only of failure to appreciate them but of failure to understand them. Freedoms vindicated anew are more precious than those achieved without effort, and only those required to justify freedom can fully understand it.

Certainly the responsibility of vindicating the claims of freedom confronts us now in urgent fashion. There have been previous examples of a challenge to freedom in our own history—the so-called Red hysteria of the early nineteen-twenties comes to mind—but we have to go back to the history of the ante-bellum South for anything comparable in scale or character to what we are witnessing today: a broad official and nonofficial attack upon nonconformity. It is unnecessary to describe this attack; its manifestations are, alas, familiar enough. It is. indeed, an awareness of the nature

and scope of that attack and of the seriousness of its consequences that has inspired this series of lectures.

How are we to vindicate the claims of freedom? More
specifically—for it is this that concerns us most nearly—how
are we to vindicate the claims of criticism and dissent and
nonconformity? There are various ways we might go about
such a vindication, some more familiar, some perhaps more
persuasive, than others. There is, for example, the constitutional or legal approach to the whole question. We could
submit the Bills of Rights, state and federal; recall the long
and glorious history of these parts of our Constitutions; cite
relevant court decisions—among them some of the most elo-
quent and moving documents in our literature. A persuasive,
even a conclusive, constitutional case could be made out
against some of the practices of state and Congressional Un-
American Activities Committees, or against such acts as the
McCarran Internal Security Bill.

Or there is what we may call the natural rights approach,
an approach which could be launched with equal effect from
experience or from theory. This approach emphasizes what
was once familiar enough to all Americans—and what we are
now in danger of forgetting—that government derives its
powers from men; that rights of life and liberty are inalienable; that these rights are not something that government
graciously confers upon men, but things no government can
take away from men. This approach is profoundly concerned
with Right—usually with individual right.

This is another way of saying that it is concerned with
what must deeply concern all of us—the dignity of man. It is
from this basic philosophical principle that the natural rights
argument derives much of its strength. For it is becoming
increasingly clear that it is respect for the dignity of the

individual that most sharply differentiates democratic from totalitarian systems. Granted this basic principle, it follows that any conduct of the state that impairs the dignity of man is dangerous. And any argument for conformity that finds its ultimate sanction in force rather than in reason strikes at the integrity of the individual, and thus at the basic principle of democracy.

But it must be confessed that neither the legalistic nor the natural rights approach to this problem of freedom is wholly satisfactory. The legal issue is almost always a bit obscure; after all, neither the Alien and Sedition Acts of the 1790's nor the Sedition and Espionage Acts of the First World War were held void by the courts, while the Smith Act of 1940 has so far been sustained. And we must, in all fairness, go even further than this. Those who are concerned for the preservation of elementary freedoms must not take refuge in legalism. It is not sufficient for freedom to be vindicated by the courts, or by constitutional experts. That is, in a sense, a barren vindication. If the preservation of our freedom depends upon the courts then we are, indeed, lost, for in the long run neither courts nor Constitution can save us from our own errors, follies, or wickedness.

Nor, for all its persuasiveness and its deep moral appeal, is the argument from natural rights conclusive. After all, it will be said, there are no rights outside society. After all, at a time of mortal danger, we cannot be too sensitive about individual rights or individual dignity—we who so readily grant the state the right to exact life and limb from our young men. After all, it will be argued, if our society and our government go under, all philosophical notions of natural rights or the dignity of the individual will be of antiquarian interest merely. Or—it will be added—concern for rights in the abstract is a sentimental luxury. "There is no right to be wrong," the Irish statesman de Valera has said, and in one form or another that attitude is widespread. Up to a certain point, so the argument runs, we can tolerate with good humor those who deny the axioms of Euclid, and we can tolerate them because they are harmless. But we do not allow them to teach mathematics. Nor do we, for example, tolerate on the highways those who insist that red is green or green is red; we take their licenses away from them.

We need not subscribe to any of these arguments to admit that they contain some elements of truth and of plausibility. The case for freedom—for freedom of dissent and heterodoxy —rests not only on these familiar and fundamental arguments, but on others as well—others that are at least equally persuasive, and that seem to me conclusive. I want to submit especially the argument of the pragmatic necessity for freedom.

*　　*　　*

Logically there might seem a deep gap between natural rights and pragmatism. The natural rights argument is transcendental; the pragmatic argument is experimental. Transcendentalism is the philosophy of absolutes; pragmatism says damn the absolute. Transcendentalism is inspired by truths that transcend truth; pragmatism will have no commerce with notions until they have submitted themselves to proof. The natural rights approach to the problem of freedom, then, establishes the principle that freedom is an absolute right and that it is an absolute good, and with these principles most of us would agree. Yet the principles are flouted or repudiated, and we must confess that they are either too complex to be understood or too weak to be effective. The pragmatic approach asks the familiar question:

What are the practical consequences of a course of conduct which denies or fetters freedom? The answer to this question will, I think, make clear that freedom is not only a right but a necessity.

Happily these two approaches to our problem are not mutually exclusive. In defiance of logic, but in response to powerful instincts, Americans have always been both transcendental and pragmatic. They have used both philosophies —used them, sometimes, interchangeably. You will find them in the first great document of our national history, the Declaration of Independence. "We hold these truths to be self-evident," wrote Jefferson, and there spoke the transcendentalist; "that whenever government becomes destructive of these ends"—there spoke the pragmatist. The alliance of transcendentalist and pragmatist persisted through the nineteenth century, in the North. The New England reformers were, most of them, transcendentalists, but it has not escaped your notice that they did not act like the idealists and transcendentalists of Germany and France and England. They acted, rather, like the utilitarians of England. They Americanized transcendentalism, put it to work, made it justify itself pragmatically. They not only insisted upon inalienable rights, but looked to the consequences of the denial of those rights—the consequences to freedom, to democracy, to the minds and souls of men. That is a large part of the meaning of the generation of 1830 to 1860—the generation of Channing and Parker, Emerson and Thoreau, Horace Mann and Margaret Fuller, Garrison and Howe and Phillips, and the others whose names still blaze like battle flags.

Nor did the pragmatists, in turn, wholly abandon transcendentalism; rather they built upon it. William James's war was not with the transcendentalists, many of whom he had loved and honored in his youth; it was with the Hegelians. Though he wanted to put every notion to the test of experience, he himself did not abandon those affluent assumptions that had so long sustained his society—assumptions about the essential virtue of man, the superiority of truth over error, of freedom over slavery.

There is, then, nothing inharmonious about combining the idealistic and the pragmatic attitudes toward the problem of freedom in our time. Nor can we, alas, assume that these two philosophical approaches to the problem are so familiar and instinctive that they need not be invoked. Past generations have preferred one or the other of these two philosophical attitudes; it has remained for ours to pay lip-service to both, and to ignore both. Uncertain of principles, we fall back on emotion; unfamiliar with the past, we guess at the future. Increasingly we tend to look to men and ideas and institutions not from the point of view of how they work, but from the point of view of how they ought to work if they fitted our *a priori* ideas about them. Increasingly we set up abstract standards and expect men and institutions to conform to them—and then judge them by the degree of their conformity. Thus we judge colleges and universities not by their actual character or by what they do but by the alleged views of their members. Thus we judge loyalty not by conduct but by gestures and ceremonies. Thus we judge organizations not by what they accomplish but by the supposed views of their members or their supposed members. Thus we judge so important an institution as the popular election of a president not by how it has worked but by our fears of how it might work—if those fears proved true. Our very politics, even our international relations, are coming to be a vulgar competition in eloquence about loyalty and rhetoric about patriotism, and we have forgotten that all those who cry Lord, Lord, shall not enter the Kingdom of Heaven.

But let us turn without more ado to the pragmatic necessity for freedom. What is the argument here? It is the argument of consequences. "The pragmatic method," William James wrote, "starts from the postulate that there is no difference of truth that doesn't make a difference of fact somewhere, and it seeks to determine the meaning of all differences of opinion by making the discussion hinge as soon as possible upon some practical or particular issue."

What, then, are the practical consequences of the attack upon independence of thought, nonconformity, dissent, which is now gathering momentum everywhere in the land? What kind of society will it create? What climate of opinion will it encourage? What will be its effect on science and scholarship, on politics and diplomacy, on security and peace? What, in short, is happening to us and what is likely to happen to us if we persist in penalizing dissent and rewarding orthodoxy?

The first and most obvious consequence is that we shall arrive, sooner or later, at an official standard of orthodoxy or —to use the current term—loyalty. It is, to be sure, one of the more curious features of the current drive against disloyalty and subversion that we so far lack definitions of either term. Yet definitions are in the making—in the making not so much by Congress or the courts, as in the minds of millions of Americans, in the daily press, in the schoolroom, in magazines and books, pulpits and forums and a thousand other vehicles and channels of opinion. If you are going to penalize disloyalty, you must first determine what is loyalty; if you are going to silence nonconformity, you must determine what is conformity—and to what it conforms. If you are going to accept J. Edgar Hoover's "easy test" of an organization: "Does it have a consistent record of support to the American viewpoint?"—you must determine what is the American viewpoint. If you are going to dismiss men from office or from teaching posts for membership in subversive organizations, you must eventually draw up a list not only of those that are subversive but of those that are patriotic. If you are going to silence dangerous ideas you must establish what are safe ideas.

To whom shall we entrust these great and delicate tasks? This is not a rhetorical question; it is an urgently practical one. Who, in our government or our society, is to determine what ideas are safe?

We need not conjure up, here, anything like George Orwell's "Thought Police," or a set of crimes like "Crime Think." It is not necessary to resort to that. The most effective censorship is not, in fact, legal; in a democracy it is—as Tocqueville pointed out—public opinion. It is not that laws may, in the end, cut us off from that body of independent and original thought that we so urgently need; it is that public opinion may create a situation where independence and originality simply do not emerge. That is even more serious. The greatest danger that threatens us is neither heterodox thought nor orthodox thought, but the absence of thought.

The second consequence of penalizing nonconformity, originality, and independence is a very practical one, and it is one whose effects are already being felt in many quarters. It is simply this: first-rate men and women will not and cannot work under conditions fixed by those who are afraid of ideas. Scholars who have to run the gauntlet of legislative investigations of their teaching, their writing, their associations, will look elsewhere for work—or will turn to purely antiquarian research. Scientists who cannot exchange information because of the requirements of security will fail to get essential information—or will refuse to work under conditions that all but guarantee ineffective and inconclusive work. Civil servants or potential government employees, faced with one investigation after another, with the overshadowing danger of smears from House or from Senate, with harassment and suspicion, will prefer employment in private industry.

It will be useful to determine, a generation from now, whether those universities that have purged their faculties are actually stronger than they were before the purges occurred—stronger in those essentials that go to make a university. It will be valuable to discover whether the civil service is, in fact, more loyal—with all the implications of that tremendous word—than the old civil service of the pre-loyalty investigation years. It will be important to know whether science advances as rapidly under the protection of security as it advanced before the days of elaborate security regulations.

A third consequence of the demand for conformity grows out of the first two. It is the development in this country of the kind of society in which freedom of inquiry does not flourish, in which criticism does not flourish, in which originality does not flourish. This is no alarmist bugaboo; it is a development already under way. Already civil servants are afraid to read certain magazines or to join certain organizations. Already teachers hesitate to discuss certain issues in class; just recently the New York City Board of Education sought to reassure them on this: you may discuss communism objectively, it said, as long as you tell pupils how wicked it all is! Already men and women hesitate to join minority parties or "dangerous" organizations, or to agitate for reform. And well they might! Just the other day we read the story of the much-decorated Negro army captain who had been asked to resign from the service because he was charged with reading the *Daily Worker* and because his father was alleged to have fought segregation in public housing. The demand was, to be sure, withdrawn. But how many instances of such official stupidity go undiscovered, unpublicized, and unchallenged? How many soldiers, duly impressed by the risks involved, were dissuaded by this episode from reading anything but the comics? Do we want the kind of army that will read only approved literature?

It is, you see, with the practical consequences to our society of the limitations on freedom that we are concerned. We do not protect freedom in order to indulge error. We protect freedom in order to discover truth. We do not maintain freedom in order to permit eccentricity to flourish; we maintain freedom in order that society may profit from criticism, even eccentric criticism. We do not encourage dissent for sentimental reasons; we encourage dissent because we cannot live without it.

* * *

Let us turn, for our illustrations, from the general to the particular. The House Un-American Activities Committee has launched an attack on the Lawyers' Guild as a pro-Communist or "subversive" organization. The chief basis for this attack is, as far as we know, that the Guild has proffered its services to the defense of Communists under indictment for violation of the Smith Act. We need not inquire into the accuracy of this charge or into the degree of zeal displayed by the Lawyers' Guild. Let us ask rather what are the logical conclusions to be drawn by the position which the House Committee has adopted? They are two: that certain criminals are so despicable that they are not entitled to counsel, and that a lawyer who defends a criminal is himself sympathetic to crime. If these principles are once officially established, what happens to the Anglo-American principle that everyone, even the worst criminal, has a right to his day in court? This principle was established not out of sentimental sympathy for criminals. It was established because it was the only way of insuring that justice would be done. If this principle goes by the board, under pressure from communism, then communism has won a notable victory; it has overturned our century-old devotion to the doctrine of due process of law.

Here is a second illustration. We read just the other day the ominous report that a Jersey City junior college had removed from its library shelves all works written by or edited by Mark Van Doren. The charge against this distinguished poet and critic was that he had associated with the wrong people; the taint of that association infected, it would seem, not only Mr. Van Doren's poetry and criticism, but Shakespeare and Milton and Wordsworth as well. The action was ominous because—if the report is to be accepted—it was taken by the faculty rather than by regents or directors.

What happened to Mr. Van Doren's books is symptomatic. Censorship of textbooks is flourishing throughout the country, though it rarely reaches the dizzy heights of imbecility attained by the Jersey City junior college. Everywhere textbooks in history, politics, and economics are under attack by "patriotic" organizations such as the American Legion or the Daughters of the American Revolution, by economic organizations like the National Association of Manufacturers and the Chambers of Commerce, or by "liberal" organizations like the National Association for the Advancement of Colored People. Whatever the animus of the attack, the principle is the same. It is the principle of censorship. It is the principle of conformity. It is the principle which assumes that truth is known, and that anything that deviates from this known truth—known to the members of the particular organization— is heresy.

Now we cannot but be indignant when injustice is done a scholar like Mr. Van Doren, and it is right that we should be indignant. Yet it is not the effect of censorship on the author or, for that matter, on the publisher, that is significant. What is significant is the effect of such censorship on our educational system—on boards of education, on superintendents, on teachers, on the boys and girls, the young men and young women, who are the end-product of the whole thing. For if you succeed in banning or censoring textbooks written by men who are critical and independent, you will get textbooks written by men who are not critical or independent, or by men who, given a choice between intellectual independence and sales, settle for the sales. If you penalize publishers for publishing textbooks by scholars who are critical, you will speedily enough persuade them to publish textbooks by writers—I do not say scholars—who are not critical. If you punish teachers for using books that organized patriots or conservatives or radicals happen to disapprove, you will get, eventually, the kind of teacher who uses the book he is told to use by the most vociferous organization. These are the people who will, in the end, direct the education of our children: writers who express no ideas because all ideas are dangerous or expensive; boards of education that are timid; teachers who are willing to conform. What kind of teaching are we going to have? What kind of students are we going to turn out? Are we going, by this method, to train a generation of students competent to deal with the difficult and complex problems of the modern world?

We may take a third example from the same arena—that of education. Let us contemplate, for a moment, the efforts of boards of regents and alumni associations and others to protect students in colleges and universities from dangerous ideas. This, too, is a nation-wide phenomenon, found alike at Harvard and at California, in Texas and in Michigan. We have, as you know, one pretty elaborate case study of this demand for conformity: the University of California. Let us look at the consequences, to that institution and to that state, of the drive for conformity.

Note, first, that we use the term "conformity." The ostensible reason for the requirement of special loyalty oaths at California was fear of communism, but that was quickly abandoned. The most elaborate investigation did not discover any Communists on any of the faculties of the University, yet the trustees did not abandon their demand in the face of this evidence, but persisted in it as a test of authority. The real issue—here as in Texas and elsewhere—was not communism but "dangerous thoughts." A prominent member of the Board of Regents, Mr. Teague, put the matter admirably in a letter to President Sproul:

I have a profound conviction that freedom in the world is being destroyed by Communism, of which Socialism is the first step. Freedom has been destroyed in England by Socialism, and the United States has travelled a considerable distance along the same line. It has been demonstrated many times that Socialism destroys incentive and reduces production.

What is most interesting here is that a member of the Board

of Regents should tell the President—and through him the faculty—what is "demonstrated" truth, and that he should insist that his own "profound convictions" are identical with cosmic laws. Clearly, if he is right, anyone who departs from his position is guilty of error—which is to say, of heresy. But if he already knows demonstrated truth in the field of economics and of politics, then the departments of economics and politics at the University are superfluous. The philosophy of Mr. Teague's argument does not differ in any essentials from the philosophy behind Nazi and Communist control of university teaching.

What have been the consequences of the demand for conformity from the Regents of the University of California? It has not rid the faculty of Communists, because there were no Communists. It has, however—and here we quote an investigation by the California Civil Liberties Union—

cost a year of horror and failure for students, teachers, and administrations; the firing of twenty-six instructors; the dropping of forty or fifty regular courses; the resignation of a large number of professors; the refusal of many well-known scholars to accept appointment; condemnation of the Regents' action by faculties of other universities and learned societies; and a general loss of confidence in the University. . . . In the long record of higher education no offense against freedom and justice has equalled in scope the ruthlessness of the offense now committed at the University.

What was gained, and what was lost? Clearly nothing was gained. But what price have the Regents paid for the luxury of their grandstand gesture against the Kremlin? The Kremlin, it may be assumed, is not seriously shaken; indeed, it must rejoice at this flattery by imitation. The important question is, what price has been paid by the scholars, the scientists, the students of the present and of the future?

On this whole matter of the teaching of "dangerous ideas" there is one observation that might well be engraved in the trustee meeting-room of every college and university. It is an observation by Whitelaw Reid, one-time owner and editor of the *New York Tribune,* and it was made in 1873:

As for the scholar, the laws of his intellectual development may be trusted to fix his place. Free thought is necessarily aggressive and critical. The scholar, like the healthy, red-blooded young man, is an inherent, an organic, an inevitable radical. It is his business to reverse the epigram of Emerson, and put the best men and the best cause together. And so, we may set down, as a . . . function of the American scholar in politics, an intellectual leadership of the radicals.

Let us turn to a fourth illustration of the attack upon independence and nonconformity: Senator McCarthy's assault upon the State Department and particularly upon Professor Lattimore and other Far Eastern experts. The Tydings Committee called these charges "a fraud and a hoax perpetrated on the Senate of the United States and the American people," but their significance goes much further than this. For we must ponder thoughtfully the consequences of McCarthy's attack and of that entire body of irresponsible criticism which finds its inspiration in the success of the Senator from Wisconsin. One consequence is that the assailants have partly succeeded in denying the State Department the confidence of the American people. Another is that American prestige abroad has suffered serious impairment. A third is that the Department is far less able to concentrate on the central task of conducting foreign relations, but must dissipate its energies on the marginal tasks of defending itself and its staff against whatever charges any Congressman may choose to bring up, for whatever reasons. A fourth is that the

Department is finding it increasingly difficult to recruit first-rate men for the important jobs it has to do. A fifth is that officials of the Department, fearful of eventual investigations, are hesitant about speaking their minds, reporting all the facts that come to them. Who knows, after all, what some future McCarthy may not do with such reports? A sixth is that hereafter experts will think twice before giving advice to the State Department and that the Department will think twice before calling in the experts. For the McCarthy charges and their aftermath established this principle: it is dangerous to give disinterested advice if anyone in Congress—or perhaps on the radio—disapproves of the advice you give. It is as if we should call in five or six doctors to diagnose an ailment, get a diagnosis of cancer, and then denounce the doctors as traitors to their oath, charlatans and marplots, and try to get them disbarred from practice. If we were powerful enough we might be successful, but we would find some difficulty in getting a doctor next time we were sick.

By denouncing as Communists or traitors those who gave us unpalatable advice, we have in a sense cut ourselves off from unpalatable advice. But that is the kind we need—almost the only kind we need; the other kind we can work up for ourselves. And the moral here is plain. If we penalize critics we will cut ourselves off from criticism. If we cut ourselves off from criticism we are likely to make mistakes. If we wish to avoid mistakes, we must create an atmosphere which encourages criticism.

Let us turn to a final illustration of the dangers implicit in the attack upon nonconformity: the present assault upon freedom of association and the rise of the odious doctrine of guilt by association. Only those familiar with Old World history can appreciate how extraordinary has been the American practice of private association. It is in many ways the most interesting and the most successful of all the institutions of democracy. The nation was founded largely by voluntary associations—the joint stock companies such as the London and the Massachusetts Bay—and from the seventeenth century to the present almost all of our major social and political institutions are voluntary organizations. Our political parties are voluntary organizations; our churches are voluntary organizations; most of our colleges and universities are voluntary associations. All of our professional, our scientific, our commercial organizations are voluntary. Indeed, the characteristic form that democracy takes in America is that of men and women banding together voluntarily to do what needs to be done. Here is where the principle of free enterprise really operates; here rather than in business.

Now, for the first time in our history, the principle of voluntary association is seriously jeopardized by the doctrine of guilt by association. It is a new doctrine. It appeared in our law only in 1940; since then it has grown and spread until this cloud, no larger than a man's hand, covers the whole horizon. Yet already its consequences are apparent. They are, in brief, that men and women are afraid to join anything. As it is dangerous to join an organization unless you know that all the other members—past and future as well as present—are above suspicion, and as it is impossible ever to know this, the easiest thing is simply to stand aloof. But once this process gets under way, democracy itself is threatened—threatened at the grass roots. For the same principle that prevents people from joining, let us say, an organization to help refugees, prevents them from joining a political party or even a church. Alexis de Tocqueville, whose chapter on

"The Use Americans Make of Public Organizations" is a classic appreciation of the role of voluntary organizations in democracy, saw this with characteristic clarity:

When some kinds of association are prohibited and others allowed, it is difficult to distinguish the former from the latter beforehand. In this state of doubt, men abstain from them altogether, and a sort of public opinion passes current that tends to cause any association whatsoever to be regarded as a bold and almost an illicit enterprise.

It is therefore chimerical to suppose that the spirit of association, when it is repressed on some one point, will nevertheless display the same vigor on all others; and that if men be allowed to prosecute certain undertakings in common, that is quite enough for them eagerly to set about them. When the members of a community are allowed and accustomed to combine for all purposes, they will combine as readily for the lesser as for the more important ones; but if they are only allowed to combine for small affairs, they will be neither inclined nor able to effect it. It is in vain that you will leave them entirely free to prosecute their business on joint-stock account; they will hardly care to avail themselves of the rights you have granted them; and, after having exhausted your strength in vain efforts to put down prohibited associations, you will be surprised that you cannot persuade men to form the associations you encourage.

This process is already under way. Every day it becomes more difficult to organize new associations, or to maintain old ones. Every day it becomes more difficult to undertake any program of reform or even of change. But the instinct for voluntary association is the instinct for democracy, and the instinct for change is the instinct for life.

It is not as if we were without experience with nations that had adopted the policy of official conformity, or with the contest between the forces of freedom and those of fear. After all, it is no accident that the nations dedicated to freedom won the two great wars of the twentieth century, and those committed to totalitarianism went under. And the more we learn about the inner history of Germany and Japan during the Second World War, the more clear it becomes that the seeds of their defeat were planted in the systems to which they were dedicated—in the suppression of criticism and dissent and the insistence upon acquiescence and conformity. Nor need we go to the Old World or to the Orient for examples; we have had experience even in our own history, and that experience is illuminating.

From about 1830 to the Civil War, the South was committed to a point of view in economics, in sociology, in politics, and in philosophy, that was all but impervious to criticism. That was the point of view that slavery was a positive good and that it was the cornerstone of a prosperous South. In defense of this peculiar institution, the South drove out, silenced, or suppressed her critics. In defense of this institution, otherwise virtuous and intelligent gentlemen burned books, banned mails, got rid of preachers who preached the wrong doctrines, got rid of editors who wrote the wrong sentiments, purged the schools and the colleges of dissenters. They were sure that they knew truth, and that all who disagreed with them or who criticized them were not only wrong but subversive. And—in part because they closed their ears to criticism and dissent—they led their section down the road to war and to ruin.

✿   ✿   ✿

We have been very busy, of late, calculating our resources and the resources of our potential enemies—and that calculation is going on all over the globe. Mr. Hoover has calculated and concluded that we do not have the strength to resist communism anywhere but in the Western Hemisphere. Mr. Kennedy has calculated and reached the same conclusion that he reached eleven years ago—namely, that our side is weak and helpless; history has taught him nothing. Mr. Taft has calculated, and he too feels that our best policy is a defensive one and that there is little use in counting on friends and associates. Interestingly enough, the German chief-of-staff, General Guderian, has published a little calculation of his own: *Can Western Europe Be Saved?* His answer is No. Russia, he asserts, has superiority in all the essentials—in manpower, in arms, in logistics, in centralization of control, in ability to command the support of her satellites. The German mind, it is clear, does not change, any more than the isolationist mind changes.

For whatever may be the balance on military resources— the atomic weapon versus manpower, logistical superiority versus air power, and so forth—there is one realm where our superiority is beyond challenge, and where it cannot be lost except by our own will. Ours is a system of freedom—freedom of inquiry, of investigation, of criticism, and of creation. Our science is unfettered. Our inventiveness is untrammeled. Our ability to inquire and criticize and resolve is unlimited. Ours is, in short, an open system, with limitless possibilites for improvement. Over against it stands the closed system of totalitarian countries. In this system, facts have to conform to preconceived ideas—or so much the worse for the facts. If biology does not justify Marx and Lenin, then you get a new biology. If music does not harmonize with Communist ideas, you reform or purge your musicians. If history does not exalt communism, you rewrite history. And if politics and diplomacy abroad do not fit into your preconceived framework, then you regard them as fraudulent and cherish your framework. This demand that facts conform to ideas extends to the whole world of affairs—to the military, the political, and the economic, as to the cultural. Thus the Communists are the prisoners of their own system. They cannot adjust their conduct to reality for they recognize only those realities that flatter their preconceptions. They cannot profit by experience for they accept only that experience that fits the pattern of their ideas. They cannot learn through criticism, for they do not allow criticism.

Ours is a different philosophy, a different tradition, and a different and happier prospect. Because we are free we can, if we will, avoid errors. We can experiment. We can criticize. We can adjust and accommodate and compromise. We can air our grievances and remedy them. Our scientists can follow where science leads. Our historians and economists can follow the track of truth. We are not committed to our mistakes. We are not committed to irretrievable errors or irreversible policies. We do not—so far—require that all those who are with us agree on everything, subscribe to a formula, follow a pattern. But we are in danger of doing just that and of forfeiting what is, in the last analysis, our greatest advantage. By insisting upon conformity in the intellectual arena and by threatening with disapproval all those who dissent or who give us unpopular advice, we are in danger of following the totalitarian philosophy—and the totalitarian errors.

It would be absurd to say that only a society dedicated to freedom can win victories. Soviet Russia is not dedicated to freedom, and she has won a good many victories. But it is correct to say that a people like ourselves, with our traditions, our history, our habits, our attitudes, our institutions of democracy and freedom, our general enlightenment, must have freedom if we are to survive. Only if we actively encourage discussion, inquiry, and dissent, only if we put a premium upon nonconformity, can we hope to solve the enormously complex problems that confront us. Only if we do this can we enlist the full and grateful support of all our people and command the respect of our associates abroad.

If in the name of security or of loyalty we start hacking away at our freedoms—freedom for the scientist, freedom for the scholar, freedom for the critic—we will in the end forfeit security as well. If the commonwealth which we cherish is to survive and prosper, we must encourage free enterprise in the intellectual and spiritual realms as well as in the economic. Our responsibility here is immense. Upon us rests, to a large degree, the future of Western civilization and of Western Christendom. If we falter here, if by silencing inquiry and criticism we fall into serious error, the whole of civilization as we know it may go down with us. We must use all our resources and use them wisely. And of all our resources, the most affluent are in the minds and spirits of free men. These we must not fritter away. At a time when we are deeply concerned with calculations of strength, we will do well to recall the closing lines of Wordsworth's sonnet, *To Toussaint L'Ouverture:*

> . . . thou hast great allies;
> Thy friends are exaltations, agonies,
> And love, and man's unconquerable mind.

Robert K. Carr

PROGRESS IN CIVIL RIGHTS

𝐼T IS NOW more than three years since the President's Committee on Civil Rights submitted its report to President Truman. In that period of time a paradoxical situation has developed. On the one hand, there has been little or no favorable action on the specific recommendations of the Committee or on the legislative program which Mr. Truman submitted to Congress in February 1948. On the other hand, however, the period has been marked by an increasing consciousness of the civil rights problem by the American people; by a growing determination that the nation should perfect its civil rights practices; by quiet, but very real progress on many fronts. During this three-year period the civil rights issue has provoked vigorous controversy, bitter arguments, and violent political quarrels. Much of the debate has been raucous and emotional, but a good part of the discussion has been reasonably calm and rational and has been centered, consciously or unconsciously, in two theses which underlie the recommendations of the Civil Rights Committee and the legislative program of the President. These two theses are: 1. a belief in the need for positive governmental action, much of it federal in character, in support of civil rights, and 2. a belief that segregation of people along racial, religious, or nationality lines must be eliminated from the American way of life.

*   *   *

I should like to cast my discussion of the civil rights problem in the form of a consideration of certain fallacies, five in number, that I think mark the arguments of those who are opposed to moving in the directions recommended by the Civil Rights Committee and the President. The first of these fallacies is seen in the oft-repeated assertion that we cannot improve the condition of our civil rights by passing laws; that we must seek progress through private, voluntary action. The fallacy here, I submit, lies in the insistence that the choice between voluntary action and government compulsion is an "either or" proposition, and that voluntary action alone can bring improvement in civil rights.

Let me make it clear at once that I do not propose to go to the opposite extreme by arguing that government compulsion must be the exclusive way of attacking the civil rights problem. No one who has studied this problem can deny the importance of private voluntary action; no one can overlook the role which education must play in strengthening our civil rights; no one can overlook the need to provide a satisfactory economic underpinning for civil rights. Where men would enjoy civil liberty, it is clear that they must, *as individuals,* understand the importance of the free way of life; they must see the folly of prejudice, bigotry, and intolerance; they must understand why they must respect their neighbors' rights if their own are to be secure. Men must also enjoy a reasonable measure of economic opportunity and security if there is to be a favorable climate in which civil liberty can thrive. But I do want to insist that there is

no need to choose between legislation and voluntary action
as though they were mutually exclusive and rival approaches
to the problem. Moreover, I should like to set forward certain
reasons why I believe legislation can help.

Let us begin by reminding ourselves that organized societies have traditionally coped with the anti-social acts of
individuals in their midst through laws enforced by government. In particular, they have used laws carrying criminal
sanctions to strike at such offenses as murder, kidnaping,
arson, and burglary. Why should we not regard civil rights
offenses as crimes against society which may properly be
defined by law and punished by government? If one man
willfully and deliberately interferes with another man's right
to vote, why should not he be punished under law?

An objection is promptly heard to such a proposal. It is said
that civil rights violations almost always have their roots in
prejudice and intolerance and that, unfortunately, a society
cannot eliminate prejudice and intolerance by passing laws.
Or to use the phrases commonly employed by opponents of
government action of this kind, it is said: "You cannot change
human nature by passing laws." "You cannot legislate morality." "Stateways cannot change folkways." Lest it seem that
I am setting up a straw man, may I point out that many
liberal and intelligent people have asserted this point of
view during the recent civil rights debate. A half-dozen
years ago when the State of New York was considering the
enactment of a fair employment practices law as a means of
eliminating racial and religious discrimination from private
employment practices, such well-known liberals as Oswald
Garrison Villard and Eleanor Herrick opposed the bill and
wrote, in a letter to the *New York Times,* "It is as impossible
to destroy prejudice and discrimination by law as it is to

control opinion or morals."[1] A little later, the one-time New Dealer, Donald Richberg, in opposing a federal FEP law, asserted, "Bad thinking cannot be legislated out of the human mind."[2] A year or so ago the *New York Times* reported that the opposition to a proposed Los Angeles FEP ordinance was being led by a local lawyer, a former president of the Los Angeles Chamber of Commerce. He was quoted as follows:

The question is . . . how best to solve the problem of people living amicably together. Shall it be by education through the schools and churches and such, in the American system, or shall we introduce the European method of coercion under the name of persuasion? This method calls first for the police and then for prison.[3]

This line of reasoning, while it carries a seeming air of persuasion, is, I believe, in the final analysis, unsound. It is a point of view based upon something less than the whole truth. It may be impossible to eliminate prejudice and intolerance through statutes. It may be impossible to change human *nature* by law. But human *behavior is* subject to social control by law. The question here is not alone whether a law can instill in people a particular moral attitude but also whether it can effectually influence their conduct. Laws against murder, for example, have not destroyed utterly the murderous drives and hatreds that take shape in some men, but certainly such laws have deterred more than one such man from putting his murderous drives and hatreds into practice for fear of the punishment that may well follow. In other words, the evil discriminatory practices that are the visible manifestation of prejudice are subject to control by law.

[1] Issue of February 13, 1945.
[2] *New York Times*, October 13, 1947.
[3] Issue of October 1, 1949.

Those who deny this fail to appreciate the role law has frequently played in history. It has been said, "Legislation, in its creative branch, is one of the most marvelous of human inventions. It would be unwise to leave the course of social life to the irrational vagaries of custom when the possibility of influencing it in a conscious and enlightened manner is given."[4] To be sure, many laws have deep roots in well-established customs. Here, long-accepted ways of doing things are carried over into formal statements of the law. But in all societies there are also examples of laws that point the way ahead. Such laws are based in firmly accepted ideals, in a people's highest aspirations, and they successfully influence human conduct even though they do not reflect past experience or actual ways of doing things. It may readily be admitted that a law which is neither based upon well-established custom nor rooted in a people's ideals will prove difficult if not impossible to enforce. The traditional illustration which is always used by those who oppose civil rights laws, the failure of the Prohibition experiment in this country, falls into this category, for it had a firm basis in neither custom nor ideal.

This is quite clearly not true of civil rights legislation. Such laws may not always be based upon established custom; but they are rooted in some of our most firmly held American ideals; they are in tune with our strongest national aspirations. Actually, it is a mistake to assert that those who advocate protection of civil rights through laws are trying to force the abandonment of private voluntary practices, because many of the discriminations against which proposed civil rights laws are directed are themselves based on law.

[4] Nicholas Timasheff, *Sociology of Law* (*Harvard Sociological Studies*, 1939), p. 311.

There are today in the United States some seventeen states as well as the District of Columbia which have laws providing for the compulsory segregation of the races. The very existence of these laws proves that the ruling classes in these states have been unwilling to let the issue of segregation be determined on a private, voluntary basis. Thus, those who oppose civil rights laws on the ground that you cannot legislate morality need to ponder the possibility that we have in fact been legislating immorality. The choice is not between "law" and "no law," nor between "law" and "private voluntary action"; the choice is between "good law" and "bad law" —between a moral law and an evil law.

* * *

The second fallacy that I want to discuss is found in the assertion that we are actually making adequate progress without law. It is argued: Congress has rejected all of the President's civil rights program. Yet the years since the Civil Rights Report was made have been marked by much progress. Ergo, private action is responsible for this gain, and it will continue to serve as an adequate basis for further progress.

Clearly, there *has been* much progress on the civil rights front in recent years. Nonetheless, there are two questions here that must be answered: *1.* Has the progress been adequate and is the rate of further progress likely to prove adequate? *2.* Has government perhaps played a part in bringing about this progress in spite of Congressional inaction?

In trying to answer the first question, we are faced at once with the difficulty of making any accurate measurements in so vast and vague a field. Signs of civil rights progress *are* numerous. The last decade has seen a very substantial decline in the number of lynchings in the United States. Negro voting in the South has increased substantially. New Mexico and Arizona have extended the suffrage to Indians. Discrimination against persons of Oriental descent has been alleviated on the West Coast in such occupational areas as agriculture and commercial fishing. The nation's armed services have made encouraging progress toward a democratic military establishment unmarred by racial and religious discrimination. The color line has disappeared from baseball. Negro police officers are found in Southern cities, Negro saleswomen in smart New York department stores. On our campuses, fraternities have made real headway in eliminating racial and religious discriminatory clauses from their charters. But it seems to me quite apparent that these signs of progress are not enough. Our country has still not had a year which has been completely free from lynching. There is still very substantial interference with the right of many American citizens to participate freely in elections. There is still much discrimination throughout our country in employment, in education, in housing, and in the enjoyment of many other social services. Segregation is still a dreadful badge of implied inferiority for more than ten per cent of the American people. It is a symbol of second-class citizenship; it is at complete war with our democratic ideals.

Any dispassionate attempt to answer the second question about the role the government may have played in contributing to progress quickly reveals that law *has* helped—that government *has* been responsible for many of the gains. For example, for some dozen years there has existed an agency in the Department of Justice known as the Civil Rights Section, which has been enforcing certain scattered civil rights statutes dating back to the legislative program enacted by Congress in the decade following the close of the Civil War. The work of this agency is clearly one of the forces that have brought about the decline in the number of lynchings in the last dozen years and the increase in voting on the part of Negroes and members of other minority groups.

Again, it is very clear that recent decisions of the United States Supreme Court have contributed to civil rights progress. There is not a shadow of a doubt that more than any other single factor such decisions have been responsible for increased voting by members of minority groups. The Southern Regional Council, in a recent report, has stated that these decisions "affirmed a principle of basic equality fundamental to American democracy. Once armed with authority, that principle could not long be defied by thoughtful Southerners without serious misgivings. As is often true in our personal lives, the South needed the force of authority to strengthen its better impulses."[5] Similarly, governmental pressure has been responsible for the admission of Negroes to graduate schools in Southern institutions, perhaps the most significant sign of progress in 1950. Indeed, it may fairly be said that this development is exclusively the result of Supreme Court action.

Or again, there are now some eight states, as well as numerous cities, that have adopted and are enforcing fair employment practice laws which make it improper for employers, labor unions, and employment agencies to discriminate in employment along racial, religious, or nationality lines. This program is all the more remarkable because these states and cities have avoided almost entirely the use of criminal sanctions in the enforcement of these laws. Instead,

[5] *New South*, September 1949, p. 7.

they have depended very largely upon negotiation, concilia-
tion, and compromise to achieve progress. Moreover, there
has here been a close integration between law and private
action in seeking the elimination of discriminatory practices.
The agencies charged with the administration of these laws
have worked closely with private organizations in an attempt
to educate people to an understanding of the importance of
guaranteeing to all men equality of economic opportunity.
It is true that such a state as New York has not become an
employment Utopia overnight. There are those critics of the
FEP program in New York who hold that it should be administered in a much more vigorous fashion; that the time
has come to use the more vigorous sanctions of the law in
cracking down upon chronic offenders. At the same time, it
is clear that very real progress is being made in states with
FEP programs—progress which would certainly *not* have
been made had not these statutes been enacted.

Finally, it should be noted that the very threat of governmental action has contributed to civil rights progress. Had
the Civil Rights Report never been made, had President
Truman not submitted a civil rights program to Congress,
and had he not continued to press for the adoption of this
program, can anyone believe that the country would have
witnessed during the last three years so much progress based
upon voluntary action?

* * *

The third fallacy is found in the oft-repeated assertion that
if we are to have any governmental action at all in support
of civil rights it should be confined to state and local levels.
Often the idea is put into words such as these: Outsiders
have no business telling the people of a community how to

handle their problems. The North has no right to try to impose a settlement of the race problem upon the South. It is presumptuous for the rest of the country to try to tell California what to do about its Orientals, or New Mexico and Arizona what to do about their Indian populations.

Again the fallacy lies in the assumption that a choice must be made between two approaches to the civil rights problem; that action must be exclusively local or exclusively national; or that the solution to the problem must be found entirely within a community or provided wholly from outside.

It should be pointed out that the Civil Rights Committee saw the need for state and local governmental action as well as for a federal program. It directed many of its recommendations to the states and communities of America rather than to the national government. However, the Committee was strongly impressed by certain arguments in support of federal action. Four such arguments may be noted. In the first place, the civil rights problem, in virtually all of its aspects, is not local but national in scope. Whenever in our history a social problem has become a nation-wide one, sooner or later the power of the federal government has been put to work to supplement state and local action. Our experience with respect to anti-trust regulation, control of labor-management relations, the elimination of child labor, or the development of a pure food and drug program all illustrate this fact. Admittedly the American civil rights problem is centered in the South. It is the civil rights of minority groups that are always most precarious. The Negro is our largest minority, and more Negroes live in the South than anywhere else. Nonetheless, the Negro problem is today by no means confined to the South. In recent decades the Negro has been leaving the South in great numbers, and as he has done so the race problem has followed him wherever he has gone until it has today become a nation-wide one. There is segregation in the North; there are Negro ghettos in the North; there have been race riots in Detroit and Chicago, as well as in Tulsa and Atlanta. Thus it is simply not true that the Negro problem is a Southern problem, and we cannot allow the Southerner to claim the exclusive right to find a satisfactory solution to the problem.

A second argument supporting federal action is that state and local public officers have been much more prone to encroach upon civil rights than have federal officers. This is a difficult assertion to prove statistically, and yet if one examines the decisions of the Supreme Court during the last quarter of a century, in which the Court has protected civil rights against encroachment by public officers, it will be found that the overwhelming majority of these cases has concerned interferences with civil rights by state and local officials rather than by federal officials. Where a state or a community is unable or unwilling to curb and discipline its own officers, I think the federal government has an obligation to act. Indeed, the Thirteenth, Fourteenth, and Fifteenth Amendments place a *specific* and *express* responsibility upon Congress to protect the rights enumerated in these Amendments against state and local interference.

A third argument for federal action is that it is inevitable that a people should attempt to use the high moral tone of the whole society in dealing with the wayward tendencies of its parts. Take the analogy of a city ward in which crime and delinquency are rampant. The city does not hesitate for a moment to use community resources and facilities in dealing with the problem. Extra police officers are poured into the ward; city-wide ordinances which reflect a higher moral tone than is to be found in the ward are invoked. In the long run efforts will inevitably have to be made to rehabilitate the ward itself and to lead the people who live there themselves to see the error of their ways. Almost certainly steps must be taken to improve economic and social conditions in the ward before a permanent solution to the problem can be obtained. But so far as the immediate threat is concerned, the city as a whole must deal promptly with the problem.

In other words, the many and varied components which make up the moral fiber of the nation give it a strength and a resiliency which cannot be matched in some of the parts. Americans *have* shown a deeper understanding of freedom and democracy and a higher regard for civil rights in the nation at large than they have sometimes shown as members of sections, or states, or communities. Should we not put that greater sense of responsibility to work in protecting our basic rights?

A fourth argument for federal action in support of civil rights arises out of the international situation. Whether we like it or not, our American civil rights record has become an international issue. Those who worked with the Civil Rights Committee saw evidence that whenever a lynching has occurred in this country in recent years, the word has echoed from one end of the globe to the other within twenty-four or forty-eight hours. People all over the world have looked to the *national* government of the United States for an explanation as to how such a shocking event can occur in a civilized country. More than that, they have looked to the national government for the taking of remedial steps to prevent recurrence of such shocking events.

More than one American diplomat, attending an international conference in recent years or working in the agencies of the United Nations, has been embarrassed in his attempts to present democracy's case to foreign lands and peoples by the reply made by his colleagues from other countries that in certain parts of the United States free elections do not exist. Such a man as Secretary of State James F. Byrnes, coming, as he did, from South Carolina, was particularly vulnerable in this respect.

Recently our attention has been called by the Supreme Court to an American civil rights problem which has had grave international significance. In the year 1913, the State of California passed an alien land law which made it impossible for Japanese aliens and other Oriental aliens in the United States ineligible for American citizenship to own or occupy agricultural lands. The law was passed in spite of the fact that three different presidents of the United States had implored the California legislature not to take such action for fear of the repercussions that might follow in Japan. Thirty-five years later the Supreme Court passed upon the constitutionality of this California alien land law and in one of the opinions in the case it is stated:

The passage of the law was an international incident. The Japanese Government made an immediate protest on the ground that the statute was an indication of unfriendliness towards its people. Indeed, the resentment was so violent inside Japan that demands were made that war be declared against the United States. Anti-American agitation grew rapidly.[6]

Who can doubt today that the passage of this law by California in 1913 was one of the things that led the Japanese people to develop a sense of unfriendliness, if not hatred, toward the United States, or was a factor in the rise

[6] Concurring opinion by Justice Murphy, *Oyama* v. *California*, 332 U.S. 633, 655 (1948).

to power in Japan of the militarists and totalitarians who led that unhappy nation down a path which brought disaster to it and misfortune to the rest of the world? Or who can be certain that similar irresponsible action by other American states or communities is not today giving similar offense to foreign peoples? We need to ponder the possibility that irresponsible action by some of our people may well do grave damage to all of us. The young man about to join the armed forces and who may be called upon to risk his life fighting a war, one of the causes of which can be traced back to the prejudiced, contemptuous policies followed by American states or communities toward their Negro citizens, their Oriental citizens, or their Indian citizens, needs to ask himself how much longer the nation at large can permit these sections to claim the right to overcome their prejudices in their own time and their own way.

As a nation in a troubled world we cannot wait for our slowest state or our most backward community to put its house in order and see to it that all freedoms are guaranteed to all its people. As we compete with communism for the friendship of colored people throughout the world—and we need here to remember that two-thirds of the world's population is colored—we must be prepared to show them that American democracy involves no discrimination against colored people; that we do not maintain a second-class citizenship for these people.

May I quote again from a report of the Southern Regional Council to illustrate the extent to which even people in the South have come to realize the need for a federal civil rights program growing out of the current international situation:

Discrimination in any part of our country works to the discredit of the whole nation in international relations . . . we must make it quite clear that our national policy is firmly opposed to discrimination of any kind. The most convincing way to demonstrate this fact is through our national Congress, which is the only body representing our people as a whole. Thus, it is at least arguable that, even when there is doubt of the complete effectiveness of a particular measure, it may be desirable as an affirmation of public policy. . . . Probably no legislation is ever passed with the unanimous support of every group in our society. Often it is necessary to defer to the wishes of a particular group rather than apply coercion. But when the national welfare is seriously involved, there should be no question of precedence: regional traditions, group interests, or whatever, should voluntarily yield to the broader necessity . . . the entire nation cannot dam back its legislative action until its most reluctant areas are persuaded.[7]

* * *

The fourth fallacy is the statement that Negroes are satisfied with segregation; indeed, that they prefer it; and that, accordingly, efforts to end it are misguided. This sort of statement is, of course, incapable of statistical measurement or disproof. Undoubtedly some of the fifteen million American Negroes are content with their segregated lot. There are, unquestionably, some Negro leaders in the South who seemingly accept segregation and who are content to argue for the maintenance of equal facilities for Negroes on their side of the line of segregation. But there is good reason to wonder whether this stand by Southern Negro leaders is not a mere matter of strategy on their part, or whether some of them indeed have not become the captives of Southern white leaders.

In general, all responsible Negro leaders and organizations outside the South are vigorously opposed to segregation and

[7] *New South,* September 1949, p. 8.

have made their position clear again and again. They regard enforced segregation as the white man's supreme insult, as the final badge of their alleged inferiority. Anyone who worked with the Civil Rights Committee and came in touch with responsible Negro leaders could not help but be impressed by their seriousness of purpose in this respect; by their sense of indignation and frustration; by their feeling of quiet desperation. In making that sort of statement I do not in any sense intend to impugn the loyalty of these Negro leaders to the American way of life. Yet plain common sense dictates that no individual's sense of loyalty to a group or a way of life should be pressed too hard where the group fails to treat him with elementary decency or justice. The Negro wants full acceptance as a first-class American citizen. He wants freedom to enter the main stream of American life. Anyone who denies that this is so is either a fool, or, what is worse, he is a knave.

Two further arguments that persuaded the Civil Rights Committee that segregation must go may be noted. The first was an argument at the level of principle. The Committee felt that segregation is contrary to the highest ideals of American democracy; in particular, to the ideal of individualism, to the belief in the integrity and worth of the individual man. If American individualism means anything, it means that we should not judge a man because of his physical characteristics or because of his membership in a racial group, matters over which he has no control and which do not affect his true worth or integrity. Instead, we should judge him in the light of his personal qualities; his ability, his industry, his willingness to coöperate, his sense of responsibility to himself and to others, and his scheme of values.

Another way of putting the same argument is to say that

segregation is immoral because it keeps people apart and prevents them from learning by experience, through living and working together, that skin color or religious belief are largely irrelevant considerations in determining a man's worth. Wherever experiments have been made in recent years in interracial activities this truth has been demonstrated. For example, a year or so ago the *New York Times* printed a statement attributed to Major General Charles W. Lawrence of the Air Force, who was reporting on the interracial experiment which was then getting under way at the Lackland Air Force Base in Texas, where some twenty-six thousand men were receiving basic training during a thirteen-week period. He said:

The integration of the base was accomplished with complete harmony. Orders went through to completely end segregation among the trainees on a certain date and when that date arrived the segregation was ended. No unpleasant incidents resulted and the white boys and the Negro boys in the training are getting along well together.[8]

In this and similar interracial experiments the findings seem to show that where men of different races, religions, and nationalities do live and work together, prejudice and intolerance begin to decline, and an understanding of the importance of the individual in his own right as against his membership in the group to grow.

To put this argument somewhat differently, we must narrow the gap between our principles and our practices, lest a sort of dry rot undermine the moral fiber of our society, lest the knowledge that we are not living up to our ideals sap our strength and stamina, or cause us to lose confidence in our own way of life. Not long ago the *Washington Post* re-

[8] *New York Times*, September 18, 1949.

ported on a state meeting of the Virginia Baptists' General Association. It seems that a committee on resolutions had submitted the following statement to the general conference for consideration and adoption:

We confess that we are prejudiced on this question [of segregation] in spite of the desires that come to us at times to be otherwise. We believe that most Baptists are likewise prejudiced. We confess that we are fearful, that we are afraid—for political, or ecclesiastical, or social reasons—to follow the way of Christ. We believe that most Baptists are likewise fearful and afraid. We confess to God our sins in this matter and plead to God to make us more willing to be Christlike in our relations to all races.[9]

Not surprisingly, the general conference refrained from adopting this resolution. Nonetheless, it reflects very well the sense of insecurity that overtakes decent people as they become increasingly aware of the gaps that remain between principles and practices in American life.

Robert Weaver has written in his volume, *The Negro Ghetto:*

Those who segregate others soon become frightened, insecure people forced to accept and invent prejudice to justify their actions. They become hypocrites who either close their eyes to stark reality or invent slogans to hide fundamental issues. The master classes, no less than the subjected, become victims of the system.[10]

And Booker T. Washington once put the same thought in these striking words, "The white man cannot keep the Negro in the gutter without getting there himself."

Secondly, the Civil Rights Committee felt that segregation must be ended because of the demonstrated fact that so-

[9] From an editorial in the issue of December 11, 1948.
[10] Robert Weaver, *The Negro Ghetto* (Harcourt, Brace and Company, 1948), p. 270.

called separate-but-equal experiments have ended in failure. The separate-but-equal policy is the best rationalization which the advocates of segregation have advanced. According to this policy it is proper to segregate people because of the color of their skin, while affording them social facilities and services equal to those made available to unsegregated peoples. The evidence is overwhelming that the facilities afforded the separated races, while indeed separate are, after more than half a century of effort, still far from equal. For example, the United States Office of Education has released statistics for the school year of 1946, which show that in the segregated school systems maintained by seventeen states and the District of Columbia, the value of school property was $250 for each white student and only $48 for each Negro student. School expenditures were $104 for each white student and $57 for each Negro student. Similar evidence is available concerning the inferior quality of the segregated services provided in such areas as recreation, transportation, housing, and health.

There has always been some doubt about the constitutionality of segregation under the equal protection of the laws clause of the Fourteenth Amendment. But in 1896, in *Plessy* v. *Ferguson,* the Supreme Court ruled that state segregation laws based upon the separate-but-equal formula met the test of constitutionality. The Court majority, speaking through Justice Brown, rejected the contention that "the enforced separation of the two races stamps the colored race with a badge of inferiority," and asserted, "if this be so, it is not by reason of anything found in the act, but solely because the colored race chooses to put that construction upon it."[11] This shocking cynicism was not allowed to pass without a

[11] 163 U.S. 537, 551 (1896).

challenge. Justice Harlan, a Kentuckian and former slave-holder, stated in a ringing dissenting opinion:

Our Constitution is color blind, and neither knows nor tolerates classes among citizens. . . . We boast of the freedom enjoyed by our people above all other people. But it is difficult to reconcile that boast with a state of the law which, practically, puts the brand of servitude and degradation upon a large class of our fellow citizens, our equals before the law. The thin disguise of "equal" accommodations for passengers in railroad coaches will not mislead anyone, nor atone for the wrong this day done.[12]

The Supreme Court has never expressly repudiated the *Plessy* doctrine, but in the last dozen years it has so undermined the ruling as to make its further usefulness to those who seek to preserve the legal basis of segregation very dubious indeed. In particular, on June 5, 1950, in three decisions, the Court struck a body-blow at the "separate-but-equal" formula. First of all, in *Sweatt* v. *Painter* it ordered the State of Texas to admit a Negro to the white law school maintained at the University of Texas and laid down such extreme conditions for the valid operation of a separate law school for Negroes as to make it virtually impossible for Texas or any state to meet them. The Court in effect said that the established graduate schools of our state universities are so unique in character and offer educational opportunities of such subtle complexity that the only way in which the test of equality can be met is by admitting all qualified applicants to them, regardless of race.[13]

Then, in the second case, *McLaurin* v. *Oklahoma,* the Court went on to say that after a Negro has been admitted to the graduate school of a white university, that university must not then segregate the Negro within its walls in such a

12 *Ibid.,* 559-62.
13 339 U.S. 629 (1950).

way as "to impair or inhibit his ability to study, to engage in discussion and exchange views with other students, and, in general, to learn his profession."[14] In other words, the Court came very close to holding that students of all races must be allowed to associate freely with one another as they go about the pursuit of their graduate studies within the same school.

Finally, in the third case, *Henderson* v. *United States,* the Court interpreted an obscure clause in the Interstate Commerce Act of 1887 in such a way as virtually to forbid segregation in interstate transportation and perhaps even to make unnecessary the enactment by Congress of one of .the laws recommended by President Truman, a statute expressly prohibiting segregation by interstate carriers.[15]

❋   ❋   ❋

The fifth and last fallacy is seen in the oft-made assertion that we must not try to move too fast in making civil rights secure for all Americans. It is said: We cannot change traditional social patterns overnight. We must first educate members of minority groups up to the responsibilities which first-class membership in American society entails. We must let these changes come in their own time and their own way. Efforts to force change too rapidly will inevitably boomerang and threaten changes that are coming as surely and as rapidly as history will allow.

Here, it seems to me, we must supplement the question, "How fast *can* we move?" with the further question, "How fast *must* we move?" It is clear that no responsible person can demand the elimination of segregation overnight. A

14 339 U.S. 637, 641 (1950).
15 339 U.S. 816 (1950).

social pattern as firmly established as racial segregation can be peacefully altered only through patient, persistent efforts. At the same time, a proper sense of the time-factor in current world affairs carries with it rather terrifying implications. We have taken eighty years—eighty rather leisurely years, I think it can fairly be said—to make the progress we have toward a final solution of our race problem. Can anyone doubt that we have today more than a very small fraction of that period of time in which to go the rest of the way to the goal?

It is being said over and over again, with great truth, that the present world conflict is essentially a struggle for men's minds. If democracy is to hold its own with communism in this appeal for the respect and loyalty of the peoples of Asia, Africa, and even South America, we cannot delay much longer in making it clear to the world that American democracy does not involve racial discrimination or interference with civil rights along racial lines. It is true that the Communists are perfectly capable of distorting the facts in this respect, and, in part, our problem is one of carrying the truth concerning our way of life to the people of other lands. But too often our continuing racial discriminations make the enemy's task all too easy. There is no need to distort the gruesome details of a photograph of a lynching, of Negro children in a dilapidated schoolhouse, or to alter the brutally frank words of a Governor Talmadge, or to exaggerate the unrelenting nineteenth-century philosophy of a Governor Byrnes. To much of the world these men speak for America. What their intransigence can do to you and me, and to our children, is almost too fearful to contemplate.

In closing, we cannot do better than to ponder the words of Prime Minister Nehru, who, perhaps more than any other statesman on the world scene today, is concerned about the growing conflict between the East and the West and its underlying basis of racial antagonism. In an address at Columbia University a few months ago, he said:

It is forgotten that nearly all the great religions of mankind arose in the East and that wonderful civilizations grew up there when Europe and America were still unknown to History. The West has too often despised the Asian and the African and still in many places denies them not only equality of rights but even common humanity and kindliness. This is one of the great danger-points in our modern world and now that Asia and Africa are shaking off their torpor and arousing themselves, out of the evil may come a conflagration of which no man can see the range of consequences.[16]

[16] *New York Times*, October 18, 1949.

Zechariah Chafee, Jr.

INVESTIGATIONS OF RADICALISM AND
LAWS AGAINST SUBVERSION

Some cynic said after the First World War that it did not teach us to love our enemies, but at least it taught us to hate our allies. The Second World War has taught us to hate each other. Never in our lifetimes have American citizens spewed such virulence against American citizens or shown such terror-stricken eagerness to shelter themselves behind novel barricades from the oft-heralded wickedness of their own fellow-countryman. This mental pestilence of hatred and fear which is raging through the land has either produced the legal devices I shall discuss or else stimulated what is old among them to feverish activity. Perhaps, like the central figures in Camus' great novel, *The Plague*, we can pull ourselves back into the attitudes of normal living and look steadily at the true dangers and needs which confront our community.

That there are dangers, I am fully aware and want to make this plain before I go any further. But they are much less new dangers than is commonly supposed. If we look closely, we shall recognize old foes with new faces. Externally, we are forced to deal with the Russian nation under absolutist rulers, as has always been the case, occupying the greatest continuous territory on earth the same as hitherto, standing apart from the thinking and historical experiences which have given our Western world its ideals of self-government and freedom, represented abroad by men unaccustomed to that give-and-take of fruitful discussion which has ripened among us through centuries of town meetings and church assemblies and legislative debates. As was pithily remarked about the Russian diplomats at the Congress of Vienna nearly a century and a half ago, "They aren't housebroken." There is nothing really new in all that. Internally, we have to reckon with considerable numbers of discontented people, but there is nothing new in that, either. Recall Shays' Rebellion, the Whiskey Rebellion in Pennsylvania, the Dorr War in Rhode Island, the Populists during the terrible dislocations in farms and factories in the nineties, and the vocal extremists of the Great Depression from 1929 to 1935. And persistent strains have been caused by the fact that a tenth of our population comes from Africa. Nobody can deny, now or in the past, that real causes for discontent do exist, but opinions are always bound to differ about the precise point where dissatisfaction becomes unfounded, and about what are the right remedies for the genuine grievances.

The novelty today is the combination between external Russia and internal discontent. Many of the dissatisfied Americans have been more or less influenced by the official political and economic philosophy of a foreign nation. But there is nothing new about that combination. Jefferson in his First Inaugural described a similar foreign influence after the French Revolution:

During the throes and convulsions of the ancient world, during the agonised spasms of infuriated man, seeking through blood and slaughter his long lost liberty, it was not wonderful that the agitation of the billows should reach even this distant and peaceful shore; that this should be felt and feared by some, and less by others, and should divide opinions as to measures of safety.

Nevertheless, we shall deal more wisely with the actual dangers presented by communism among discontented Americans if we refuse to adopt the attitude of the Preamble to the McCarran Act, which completely identifies American Communists with the aggressors in the Kremlin. This would treat all Americans who knowingly become Communists and many of those joining "Communist front" organizations simply and solely as participants in a secret conspiracy to establish totalitarian dictatorship everywhere; "in effect," the Preamble declares, they "repudiate their allegiance to the United States and transfer their allegiance to the foreign country in which is vested the direction and control of the world Communist movement."

I doubt if this be true of all such persons, and anyway it is only a small aspect of the problems presented by American Communists. They are not only Communists; they are Americans too. They are linked with the lives of nonradical Americans in many ways, most of which have no relation to whatever revolutionary views they entertain. We shall reduce their harmfulness much more successfully if, for a while, we stop being terrified by abstract phrases about a vast international conspiracy and just think of these persons as an American problem. Here are some sixty or seventy thousand people in our midst, with ideas considerably at odds with the rest of us. Instead of tearing ourselves to pieces with fears of what a vague mob with a hated label may do to us in the future, it will be wise to look at them as individual men and women here and now. They are "American problem children." What made this man and that girl become a Communist in the first place? What is he or she like when not going to party meetings or handing out pamphlets? Goethe said: "It is a wise maxim of governments not to deal with men as they ought to be [or ought not to be], but as they are."

*　　*　　*

Once we start looking at American Communists as distinct human beings—as annoying and possibly dangerous fellow-citizens and not a mob of ogres—we may find it as absurd to assume that all of them are alike as that all businessmen are alike. The callow college boy whose radicalism leads him into a Communist Youth Society may be as far apart from the editor of the *Daily Worker* as Senator Ralph Flanders is from Tom Girdler. There is an enormous flow out of the Communist Party, typified by Arthur Koestler and other authors of *The God That Failed,* and also by Professor Budenz of Fordham, Whittaker Chambers, and Elizabeth Bentley. These reformed revolutionists are conclusive proof that there is a great variety among the kinds of discontented individuals who become Communists. Many of them can clearly be reclaimed if effective counter-influences are brought to bear, but that cannot be accomplished by legal measures which oust them from every sort of work for which they are fitted and trained, thereby leaving these Americans with nothing to do for the rest of their lives except to be embittered agitators. The true remedy is to bring these discontented men and women out of the muddy backwaters into the clear currents of national life, to turn them into loyal citizens. It is the task of a wise psychiatrist—to reach isolated and perplexed minds and bring them into renewed communication with their fellowmen.

Surely, that task can best be accomplished if we leave

these disaffected men as free as the rest of us to make their grievances known, if we constantly try to reduce the inequalities and hardships of which they justly complain, and also endeavor to persuade them that sometimes they are asking for better bread than is made of wheat. Many of these extremists are young, and youth is a fault everybody outgrows.

Above all, the way to make men love their country is to give them a good country, imperfect like everything else in this world, but where the shortcomings are getting constantly recognized and then removed. And it must be a free country. The great revolutions in history were in Bourbon France and Czarist Russia, nations completely equipped with sedition laws and censorship. The countries which have inspired men's utmost devotion have been free countries—Athens, Switzerland, Holland, and our own while it stood firmly by the ideals of Jefferson and the First Amendment. The only way to preserve "the existence of free American institutions" is to make free institutions a living force. To ignore them in the very process of purporting to defend them, as frightened men now urge, will leave us little worth defending.

Yet I do not deny that there may be some incurably disaffected American Communists. They cannot be reclaimed, but then the true task is to find the best ways of lessening their capacity to do really harmful acts. Here again the illusion of uniformity and the blind terror of a single world-wide conspiracy will unfit us for devising effective remedies for this perplexing internal problem. I think that we shall be wise to approach it just as we would a baffling problem in biology or mathematics. Break it down into separate parts and then go at each part in temporary isolation.

Using this breakdown method, let us set apart those American Communists who are in fact emissaries of the U.S.S.R., bent on spying and sabotage in this country, and deal with them as we would with any spies or saboteurs, through the Federal Bureau of Investigation and regular criminal trials and the customary agencies of our government. There is abundant legislation for this purpose on the statute books; it punishes espionage of all sorts, and molestation of property of every kind; and persons who have not yet committed wrongful acts but are serving as agents for foreign governments or engaging in political activities here "subject to foreign control," can be forced to register under laws enacted in 1940. We can reach in this way anybody who is really carrying out orders from the Kremlin, without behaving as if the meeting at Peekskill to listen to Paul Robeson was an overseas session of the Politburo.

Isolate the problem of Communist Negroes, and study it as a part of the whole Negro problem. The question of what to do with extremists from this race is just a fringe of the whole complex of racial relations.

Look at radical teachers in relation to the purpose of education, and then you will not wholly forget how inspiring communication of ideas to the young depends on maintenance of the American ideal, which Jefferson proclaimed at the University of Virginia: "This institution will be based on the illimitable freedom of the human mind. For here we are not afraid to follow truth wherever it may lead, nor to tolerate error so long as reason is left free to combat it."

The one spot where Communists might do the greatest harm in this country seems to me to be by infiltrating labor unions. A few fanatical workmen could shut off the entire supply of water or electric power from a great city. Even so,

I believe that we shall best guard against such dangers by looking at Communist labor leaders as part of American labor problems. Trade unions are an essential element in our industrial life, and yet they frequently perplex us by choosing leaders who are ready to defy the courts and even the President in order to further what they believe to be vital interests of workmen. Communist labor leaders are only a recent manifestation of the radicalism and lawless tendencies which have always existed to some extent in the labor movement alongside the indispensable functions performed by unions. The motives of Communist union officials may have a closer resemblance to those of John L. Lewis, Petrillo, and the labor men who recently walked out of government mobilization boards, than to the plots of Josef Stalin. At any rate, it would be profitable to consider the anti-Communist oath in the Taft-Hartley Act in connection with industrial problems rather than as an annex to the Smith Act and the McCarran Act.

I fully realize that this breakdown method ignores a certain amount of interconnection between these separated problems of American discontented radicals, but nevertheless I believe that we shall get much further in the solution of these problems in the manner described than if we huddle them all together in a vast nightmare of the World Communist Movement.

*   *   *

Now, I pass to another argument for drastic treatment of radical American citizens—not only Communists, but also men whose talk, reading, or associations depart from what is rapidly becoming the American party-line. The defense is put forward on behalf of the registration provisions in the McCarran Act and proposed purges of schools, colleges, government departments, and the bar, that our present troubles are just the prelude to a Third World War. Hence we must close up our ranks for the terrible struggle ahead. The slightest possibility of disloyalty, or even of doubt as to the nobility of all our aims, would be as fatal as on a battleship with the enemy fleet coming over the horizon.

This conception of thought-control as an indispensable instrument of victory was not held by Washington on Cambridge Common, by Lincoln after Fort Sumter, or Franklin Roosevelt after Pearl Harbor. It was not even held by Woodrow Wilson in 1917 despite his suppression of a good deal of discussion under the Espionage Acts; and that is now recognized as a bad mistake by ardent supporters of far greater suppression in 1951. But this time, we are told, it will be total warfare against totalitarians and only totalitarian methods can save us. A good deal of the public willingness to send people either to unemployment or to a federal prison, without their having done anything which was ever a crime before, stems from the emotional conviction that we are in a pre-war period.

Nobody can say we are not. A reader of Thucydides remembers how the conflict which shattered Greek civilization began with a civil war in Corfu, a region remote from either Athens or Sparta. Our Corfu may be Korea. The parallel is persuasive, and yet it may be false. Instead of being pre-war, the present anxious disturbances may be post-war. The true parallel may be at the other end of the Peloponnesian War, when the slowly recovering Athenians tried thought control on Socrates. At any rate, I believe that we can understand many of our troubles better if we regard them, not as a prelude to a fortunately uncertain Third World War, but as the aftermath of the Second.

After every great war there has to be a shakedown. Our Civil War, for example, kept the nation in a turmoil until 1877 at least. The shakedown, always a disagreeable process, is worse than ever this time because six perplexing factors are operating together and four of these are disastrous. *First,* the devastation and dislocation of the customary processes of civilized life. We must go back to the Thirty Years War for a parallel to the ruined cities, the destruction of slowly replaceable farm animals, the multitudes of homeless and starving people both in Europe and China. *Second,* the disappearance of previous governments from many regions, such as Palestine, India, and Korea. After the Peace of Westphalia, after Waterloo, princes and parliaments were on hand to resume customary tasks. Even in 1918, although great nations had dissolved, former political leaders and local governments survived to pick up the pieces. Now there are hardly any pieces and none of the old authorities to pick them up. Unless men on the spot in the abandoned outposts of empire display unusual courage, wisdom, and restraint, their territory is sure to be afflicted by internal disorders and eyed by powerful neighbors. *Third,* the conflict between ideologies. Westerners and Soviet Russians are as far apart as Greeks and Persians, or Christians and Mohammedans. Post-war settlements would have been hard enough without this novel complication. At Versailles, with the Russians frozen out, men reared in the long traditions of European civilization failed to build a durable peace. Now it has to be done with the Russians very much in and thinking quite differently from ourselves. *Fourth,* the discovery of the atomic and hydrogen bombs, which in the hands of aggressors or a few lunatics are capable of wiping out civilization and perhaps the human race.

The two remaining factors offer hopeful possibilities, but they raise very difficult problems, of which the United States had no previous experience to serve as guidance. One such novel factor is that several enormous peoples of Asia have suddenly emerged into national strength. *Finally,* our country finds itself for the first time a member of a world-wide organization, in which we are constantly called upon to co-operate with other nations, whose wishes sometimes differ from ours. We have been accustomed to go it alone in our foreign policy, but now we are asked to mold it so as to take account of criticisms, disagreements, and opposition. It is never easy to talk wisely while violent action is taking place, and it is especially hard to do so in an organization which is in the early stages of growth.

Mankind and our own country have never had to face so many baffling challenges simultaneously. And most of these challenges seem likely to make great demands upon us for a long time to come.

*   *   *

It should be obvious to every American citizen that, in order to meet these challenges successfully, the country needs more than ever before public servants and government advisers who will do vigorous independent thinking about novel problems. The same mental qualities are demanded by the growing complexity of the purely internal tasks of federal and state governments. They are equally necessary in teachers at all levels, if they are to prepare young Americans to take an effective part in solving difficulties a few years ahead, whose exact nature it is impossible to foresee. Adults, too, need to be helped; only through plenty of un-trammeled discussion in books, magazines, newspapers, and meetings of organizations do we arrive at a healthy under-standing of our difficulties and of the merits of competing solutions.

The tragedy is that the very same factors which make vigorous and independent thinking indispensable have been operating to create popular tensions and fears which more and more discourage such thinking in the very places where it is most needed, among public servants, teachers, and the unofficial molders of public opinion. Owen Lattimore did his own thinking, and look how his services were appre-ciated. Even after all the charges against him proved to be unsupported by any evidence and after he was cleared by a Senate committee, a considerable number of American citi-zens, including many graduates of Wellesley, maintained that it was unsafe to let him talk in public about matters which he had investigated for years. Remember the repeated interruptions to the scientific work of Dr. Condon. Think of the effect of such rewards for public service upon other loyal government workers, when offered the opportunity to leave Washington and take more lucrative private employment. High officials are already asserting that it is increasingly difficult to recruit promising young men for important gov-ernment jobs. Men who could do notable service for the country are going elsewhere rather than enter the poison gas of endless suspicions, eavesdropping, and Congressional browbeating which hangs over the City of Washington. The same process is under way among teachers, especially in public schools and state universities. Eminent scholars are refusing to teach at the University of California, which until a year ago was probably the most distinguished among state universities, because it has discharged a score of its leading scholars after years of devoted service. The very men who voted to dismiss them expressly stated that these professors were loyal. The only cause for cutting short their honorable careers was their refusal to make a formal assertion of qualities which there was never any reason to doubt.

Hundreds of thousands of men and women whose job it is to think are objects of hostility to the citizens they serve. They are working in an atmosphere of suspicion and under the risk of losing their jobs, not because of any crime or professional misconduct in the past, but because people are afraid that they might do something wrong of an indefinite nature at some vague time in the future. Loss of a government job or a teaching position on grounds of disloyalty ruins the man's chosen career and renders it very difficult for him to support himself and his family in some other occupation for which he is wholly untrained. Employers are not going to hire him. Dismissal under such circumstances is punishment of a severe kind.

*   *   *

It is something quite new to punish men drastically who have done nothing wrong, merely for fear that they might do something wrong. Such a practice is wholly alien to the traditions of English-speaking freedom. Those traditions were ably set forth by Justice Jackson in a recent decision, which extended bail for the eleven Communists convicted in New York in 1950. The government was urging that they ought to go to prison right away, although their case was still to be decided by the United States Supreme Court. It was said that they might do serious harm if they were left at liberty during the appeal. Justice Jackson said:

If I assume that defendants are disposed to commit every opportune disloyal act helpful to Communist countries, it is still difficult to reconcile with traditional American law the jailing of persons by the courts because of anticipated but as yet uncommitted crimes. Imprisonment to protect society from predicted but unconsummated offenses is so unprecedented in this country and so fraught with danger of excesses and injustice that I am loath to resort to it.

Nevertheless, we are more and more punishing people in this country for possible future wrongdoing. The thing began with the formation in 1938 of the House Committee on Un-American Activities, which broadcast ill-tested rumors about the loyalty of scores of citizens, who were not present to defend themselves and who, with no criminal acts either charged or proved, were punished more severely than if they had been fined, because "a good name is better than riches" and some of these lost their cherished jobs as well. And the Committee has sent 'many men to jail, too, for no greater injury to society than refusing to answer questions which were equally unrelated to anything ever a crime before this Committee set to work. Its Un-American Activities did, indeed, start before the Second World War, but their range and recklessness in ferreting out men who might conceivably do some bad acts some day increased with post-war excitement. Now the Senate, which long stood aloof in contemptuous silence, is trying to outdo the House.

A very different way of penalizing wrongdoers before they did any wrong came as an accompaniment of war-time fears, with the removal of thousands of American citizens of Japanese descent from their homes and businesses in California, Oregon, and Washington to concentration camps in the desert, without any investigation to prove past misconduct or even present disloyalty. The only ground was the chance that some of them might have the kinds of minds which would make it conceivable that they might some day commit spying or sabotage. The next step was the federal loyalty investigations, where a man who had faithfully performed his official work for years under the eyes of his superiors and associates was nevertheless considered an object of suspicion because he might do something wrong some day. The same thing has been going on for schoolteachers and college professors. Distinguished leaders of the bar are urging the purge of lawyers in every state who might do something wrong. Under the McCarran Act, American citizens can be interned in wartime by government officials who think that they might conceivably do something wrong.

Possibly the country is in such dire straits that we need to adopt this wholly new policy of punishing offenses before they are committed without knowing that they ever will be committed. At least we should realize that we are doing something entirely new in the name of security. Certainly we should scrutinize every new proposal of this sort with the utmost care and measure how far we are departing from the freedoms for which we are urged to fight. If these novel measures are in fact warranted by the emergency, then we ought to limit them to the emergency and be absolutely sure that they come to an end when the emergency is over.

*   *   *

Meanwhile, what course lies open to patriotic Americans who love their country because of the great freedoms in the

Bill of Rights and want them maintained as fully as possible during these troublous times? Let me start with Congressional committees. Is their function to be investigation or invective?[1]

The special problems presented by the Un-American Activities Committee of the House are only part of much broader problems raised by the whole subject of Congressional investigations. Their extensive use is rather recent. Such committees were comparatively powerless to compel witnesses to answer questions until the Supreme Court, during the Teapot Dome affair, upheld the right of Congress to range widely while collecting evidence in order to ascertain what is best for the national welfare. Consequently, even though the First Amendment is involved, the Supreme Court is not likely to do much interfering with the kind of legislative investigations with which we are concerned. Judges are naturally reluctant to tell Congress how to do its own job.

Yet this does not mean that Congress ought to do whatever it can do. If the courts refuse to impose constitutional limitations on probes into men's opinions and intellectual associations, then the responsibility is put on Congress to work out wise limitations for itself and put an end to abuses and unfairness on the part of its own committees. Justice Holmes said that "legislatures are ultimate guardians of the liberties and welfare of the people in quite as great a degree as the courts." Usually Holmes's words are taken as a directive to judges to keep hands off, but they are also an exhortation to Congress and the state legislatures to resume their

---

[1] The following paragraphs, dealing with Congressional investigations, were included in Professor Chafee's Foreword to Alan Barth, *The Loyalty of Free Men* (New York: The Viking Press, 1951), pp. xi-xviii. They are reproduced here with the permission of the publisher.

great traditional task of protecting the ordinary man from governmental oppression.

Congress has the obligation of reshaping the procedure of investigating committees so as to give a citizen rights approximating those which the Constitution gives him in a criminal trial. And when Senators or Representatives baselessly slander decent citizens on the floor and in committee rooms, the fact that the Constitution exempts them from paying damages in court ought to make the Senate or the House alert to punish such baseless statements itself. The constitutional provision that "for any Speech or Debate in either House, they shall not be questioned in any other Place" ought to be read, as it rarely is, in connection with the preceding words of the Constitution, "Each House may . . . punish its members for disorderly Behaviour. . . ."

The two outstanding points about legislative investigating committees are that they are well suited to pass on general questions and badly suited for the decision of individual cases. By general questions I mean the collection of large masses of information which may show the need for new statutes and how new laws ought to be wisely drafted. And I mean more than preparation for legislation. These committees enable Congress to review the past expenditure of vast sums of taxpayers' money and to keep a constant watch upon the conduct of public officials. This last matter is especially important today because of the great number of federal employees and the wide range of their activities. The people whose lives are affected by these multitudes of unelected officials have no control over them except through their chosen representatives in the Senate and the House. Such far-flung functions as I have been describing could easily be hampered by judicial interference. Congress should be free to choose the ways for carrying out these important tasks. That is what Congress is for.

On the other hand, Congress was not designed to determine whether an individual is innocent or guilty of crime or other misconduct. That is what courts are for. Hence the constitutional prohibition of bills of attainder. And a Congressional committee is just as unfit for this task as the whole House. In certain special situations a court may be replaced by an administrative tribunal equipped as far as possible with the impartiality of a judge, but that is the sole proper alternative way of trying citizens for offenses. Senators and Representatives cannot be expected to display impartiality. Everything they do in the day's work runs in just the opposite direction. The Constitution does allow them to conduct one kind of trial—an impeachment, and what happens then is very significant. President Johnson escaped removal by one vote, but today the evidence against him seems utterly flimsy. This is a striking proof of the unavoidable influence of purely political considerations on Congressional determinations of the guilt of an individual. Party policies and the desire for reëlection cannot be excluded from the minds of Senators and Representatives. "We have been unearthing your New Dealers," said the Republican chairman of the Un-American Activities Committee. Judges are kept impartial by professional training, the customary safeguards of the courtroom, and the ingrained traditions of the bench. No such factors operate on the men who sit in the Capitol. They are sent there by the people to do a very different job from that of judges, a job that demands very different qualities. Consequently, Congressmen and Senators should, as far as possible, keep away from the judges' job of passing on the guilt of individuals.

If we apply these two points to a committee investigating the possibility of disloyal government officials, for instance, in the State Department, the proper work of the committee is to look at the loyalty program as a whole and to furnish Congress and the public with a set of general conclusions about the way that program is actually administered. Are the methods used efficient to detect really bad people and do they furnish adequate protection to the innocent? What better methods can be suggested? Such a general survey is peculiarly within the capacity of Congress, which is concerned with both the welfare of the nation and the liberties of all the citizens. But when the Congressmen on a committee get away from a general review of methods and undertake to reverse or affirm the decision of a loyalty board in a single case, as if the committee were an appellate court, then questions of innocence or guilt are submerged in partisan battles. Moreover, the committee's disagreement with the outcome of an individual case is not good proof that this case was wrongly decided. Every student of law knows that two different judges or juries frequently disagree about close issues. The purpose of the double-jeopardy clause in the Constitution is to protect a released prisoner from this very fact. When an acquitted man cannot be forced to undergo a second trial before a jury, his second trial before a Congressional committee is surely abhorrent to American traditions.

Of course there cannot be a rigid rule wholly excluding individual cases from consideration by an investigating committee. Sometimes elaborate examination of particular actions is indispensable to establishing a general conclusion. The Teapot Dome investigations showed this. But this task, if it has to be undertaken, calls for special caution and restraint on the part of the committee. When individual cases do have to be brought in, they should be regarded as incidental to the review of a general situation and not as ends in themselves. Congress sits to make laws for everybody and to supervise administrative methods for everybody. It is not its business to pass judgment on one man, except by impeachment.

Matters are still worse when the committee undertakes to investigate thought and speech in private life, as in the notorious hearings to discover objectionable features in motion pictures. Congressmen are even less fitted to be dramatic critics than they are to be judges.

When a Congressional committee does find itself obliged to examine an individual charged with disloyalty, for the sake of settling some general policy or procedure, then the first thing to remember is that the committee is, for the time being, charged with the same responsibilities as a court. Although it has not the same power as a judge and jury to send men to jail, it is able to impose different and very severe punishments. It can smear a man's reputation grievously, and to many men a good name is as important as merely being out of jail. The committee can also do a good deal toward depriving the men whom it condemns of their jobs, whether they be government officials or Hollywood writers. Nor does the committee lack the power to imprison men. It can send them to jail for refusing to answer questions, even those which decent people would not ask.

A committee which possesses so much of the power of a court ought to behave like a court. When its members see fit to be judges of a particular individual, they should try as hard as they can to overcome the political partialities which (as I have pointed out) differentiate Congressmen from real judges. At least their proceedings should have the formality prevailing on the floor of the House and of the Senate. It is high time to throw out the kleig lights, the cameras, and television. They hinder calm determination of the fate of the accused person just as much as they would in a courtroom, and they destroy the dignity which ought to be displayed by the chosen representatives of the American people, sitting to discharge a grave public duty.

It is not enough, moreover, to imitate the outward qualities of a court. Still more important, the procedure for deciding an individual's guilt or innocence in a committee should seek to approximate the safeguards against bias and error which prevail in criminal trials.

Here is a problem for statesmen. The history of criminal trials brings out the nature of their task. Go back three or four hundred years, say, to the trial of Sir Walter Raleigh or the Earl of Essex, and you find a startling lack of our commonplace decencies for determining guilt. The prisoner was browbeaten by judges as well as prosecutors. He had no lawyer. He was not allowed to call any witnesses, much less compel them to appear. He could not testify on his own behalf. It took centuries of struggle and hard thinking to obtain impartial judges and to work out the civilized procedure for trials in a courtroom embodied in our Sixth Amendment:

In all criminal prosecutions the accused shall enjoy the right to a speedy and public trial . . . and to be informed of the nature and cause of the accusation; to be confronted with the witnesses against him; to have compulsory process for obtaining witnesses in his favor, and to have the assistance of counsel for his defense.

Now the nation is starting a new kind of tribunal—Congressional committees. Nobody has really thought about working out a civilized procedure for them. So sometimes their investigations have a good deal of resemblance to criminal trials in 1600. Harlow Shapley was questioned in secrecy by the Un-American Activities Committee, his lawyer was forcibly ejected from the room, he could call no witnesses, his written statement was torn from his hands by the presiding member of the committee. On other occasions there has been far too much publicity, amounting to a mob in a courtroom. Congress should be ashamed to let this go on any longer. Perhaps a committee hearing which can ruin or clear a man's reputation ought not to be an exact counterpart of a criminal trial. All the more need for Congress to get to work and plan what different safeguards should be provided for the innocent man. The First Congress formulated decent procedure for criminal trials in federal courtrooms. The Eighty-second Congress ought to give us a decent procedure for this new device for punishing an individual in its committee rooms.

Just how far it is wise for a Congressional inquiry to imitate a criminal trial cannot be stated offhand, but the person summoned for questioning should surely be allowed to bring in his own lawyer. He needs him badly, to advise him about improper questions and perhaps about his right to refuse to incriminate himself. The Un-American Activities Committee has defended its occasional denials of the right to counsel by comparing itself to a grand jury, into which the witness goes unaccompanied. Yet the situation is obviously different—the grand jury insists on secrecy in order to protect innocent persons, whereas, even when committee proceedings are held in secret, some member issues a statement to the press relating the smears of the day. The right to cross-examine hostile witnesses raises more difficulties. Perhaps the way out is to allow the lawyer of the accused to suggest questions to be asked by the chairman, and for the chairman to have the honesty to disclose discreditable facts in the past careers of the witnesses on whom the committee relies. At least the defense should be able to bring in witnesses in order to attack the credibility of the man who has been telling damaging stories about the accused. The situation now is what Alan Barth calls an "open-house invitation extended by legislative investigators to every renegade Communist and stool pigeon . . ." And common decency should allow the accused to produce other testimony in his own defense, within reasonable limits. Moreover, he is fairly entitled to some sort of specification of the lines of inquiry well ahead of the hearing, so that he may prepare an adequate defense. He ought not to be obliged to come into the committee room knowing nothing of what it is all about, and then be forced to answer questions roving over his whole life, or else go to jail if he prefers to preserve his privacy.

So much for the rights of the person actually before the committee. Serious harm can be done, as well, to a man who is not in the room at all. Suppose a former Communist takes the stand in Washington and accuses Mr. Jones, a reputable citizen in New York City, of having been an active member of the Communist Party. The afternoon newspapers spread the charge on their front pages. Mr. Jones is helpless. Weeks later he may have a chance to appear himself and reply, but by that time the matter is cold. Some war scare or another political scandal is on the front pages. Most of the readers who saw the charge do not see the reply. The mud sticks, and there is nothing he can do about it. Surely there must be some remedy for this gross unfairness. The committee's counsel knows what the ex-Communist is going to say long before the hearing. So there is time for him to give Mr. Jones advance information of the general nature of the future testimony against him. Then, Mr. Jones should be allowed to appear before the committee on the same day as his accuser, or at least to file a brief reply to his accuser; and the committee should do its best to make sure that the reply is printed by the newspapers in the same issue as the damaging charges against Mr. Jones.

Finally, the members of the investigating committee might try to behave like judges after the committee session is over. No self-respecting judge expresses opinions about a pending case, either to the press or in public addresses. Contrast the uncontrolled revelations by the Un-American Activities Committee while evidence is going in.

Some people may think it makes no difference what methods are employed by this committee—the sufferers are "Communists" anyway. But public opinion is capable of rapid shifts to fresh objects of excited detestation. Instead of radicals, businessmen may easily become the target of investigation, as has frequently happened in the past. Suppose the methods now employed by the Un-American Activities Committee were taken over by a Congressional committee investigating monopolistic practices or high prices of the necessities of life. Suppose a prominent manufacturer is grilled about all his private economic and political opinions. Suppose he is ordered, like the Anti-Fascist Refugee Committee, to bring all the ledgers and all the correspondence files of his organization several hundred miles to Washington. Suppose he is given no lawyer, no chance to cross-examine the psychopaths who accuse him of nefarious schemes to starve the poor, no opportunity to present testimony of his own to discredit these witnesses and establish his own innocence.

The only real remedy for abuses by investigating committees lies, not in the courts, but on the floor of Congress.

      ✿   ✿   ✿

What can wise and loyal Americans do about the Internal Security Act of 1950, commonly called the McCarran Act?

This extraordinary combination of several separate bills on different aspects of disloyalty does to a slight extent punish acts which have long been regarded as criminal by nature. For instance, gross negligence by a government official in permitting the theft of documents from a research laboratory or failing to make a prompt report of their disappearance is plainly a dereliction from duty. If it was not previously a crime, the increasing importance for defense of atomic and other scientific research makes it prudent to correct the oversight. For the most part, however, the Act either creates entirely new kinds of criminal activity or else penalizes men for fear they might do some bad acts some day. Since the last is its main purpose, the Act is the gravest departure yet from the principle, declared by Justice Jackson, that "the jailing of persons by the courts because of anticipated but as yet uncommitted crimes" is "fraught with dangers of excesses and injustice" and "difficult to reconcile with traditional American law." In view of the fact that the Act was opposed by the Department of Justice, the Department of Defense, the Central Intelligence Agency, the Department of State, and Mr. Truman, the Commander-in-Chief of all our armed forces, who considered it seriously damaging to national security measures, the statement by

Congress, over and over again in the Act, that this legislation was "necessary" to meet the "clear and present danger" created by the world Communist movement, is not impressive. Perhaps there was no need for the Senators and Representatives to save the country, but they did want to save their seats.

The McCarran Act falls roughly into four parts. One part, of which I have already spoken, allows the large-scale internment of citizens (whites as well as Orientals this time) in concentration camps on the outbreak of war. Here everything depends on who is Attorney General.

A second part creates the novel crime of any act which would substantially contribute to the establishment in the United States of a foreign-controlled dictatorship. Mr. Truman, in his veto message, inquired what "substantially contribute" means, and concluded: "A phrase so vague raises a serious Constitutional question." Here again, prosecutions are unlikely unless we have a different kind of Attorney General from J. Howard McGrath.

Another part relates to immigration. It requires the exclusion or deportation not only of foreigners who are definitely shown to be bent on dangerous acts, but also of many new kinds of bad minds which might somehow or other lead to bad deeds. For example, it keeps out of the country anybody who is or was a member of or affiliated with any organization which advocated any form of totalitarianism. The foreigner may not have belonged for years—it is enough if he "ever has been" connected with such a group. No visa can be issued to such a foreigner, and anybody who helps him get into the country is severely punishable.

Here is how this law is already working. A young American citizen, descended from the best native stock on both sides, met a young Czech woman. When the Nazis occupied her country in 1939, her father was thrown out of his professorship and denied the chance to support his family in any other way. She, a girl of sixteen, went to work in a factory in order to keep herself and her parents alive. She had to join a trade union to get the job. Of course, it was a Nazi trade union. Later she went to a concentration camp. Before the Communists replaced the Nazis, she escaped to Frankfort. The American Occupation Government picked her out with other promising girls for study at an American college. She and the American young man fell in love and married in August, two days before she had to return to Germany to report to our Occupation Government the results of her American studies, in accordance with the terms of her agreement. Before she left, she was promised a return visa and engaged a westward passage on October 10th. On September 23rd the McCarran Act became law. Our consul in Frankfort refused the visa as Congress had ordered. Her husband has written to everybody in Washington. Everybody says "What a pity!" and nothing happens. And so, as the McCarran Act says, "to preserve the sovereignty of the United States as an independent nation," a promising American citizen cannot have his wife with him.

Even Senator McCarran is shocked by this kind of incident. He says the Administration ought not to enforce the law so vigorously. Mr. McGrath could undoubtedly make use of a proviso for temporary visits by these compulsorily Nazified youngsters, but a wife is not a visitor. And if he did employ this proviso freely, Senator McCarran would be the first to complain that he was thwarting the intentions of Congress and swamping us with totalitarians. You're damned if you do, and damned if you don't!

The consequences of the hostility to unfamiliar foreign ideas in this and earlier immigration statutes go far beyond these cases of individual hardships, bad as they are. Many notable contributions to the thought and literature of the world have been made by men who wrote or published in countries not their own. It suffices to mention Dante, Locke, Montesquieu, Voltaire, Rousseau, Heine, Mazzini, and Tom Paine. Furthermore, the ability of the people of one country to learn contemporaneously about the people of another country depends greatly upon the ease with which journalists are allowed to pass international frontiers and upon the extent to which news flows back and forth across these frontiers.

The values just described will be hard to attain if governments are inhospitable to visiting thinkers and writers on the ground of their opinions. Consequently, the manner in which a nation exercises its power over immigration and expulsion can either promote or fetter freedom of thought and expression.

One difficulty is that the general immigration laws of a nation like ours are sometimes primarily designed to determine the character of its permanent population. The restrictions are framed with regard to aliens who wish to settle in new homes and become citizens. Yet restrictions suitable for these intending settlers may be unsuitable for temporary visitors whose coming would further the international exchange of news and ideas. The application of a single set of restrictions to settlers and visitors alike raises obstacles to freedom of information. These obstacles do not seem to be satisfactorily removed by the practice (already mentioned) of exceptional official dispensations for some temporary visitors who cannot be lawfully admitted as permanent settlers. Such special favors are not sufficient recognition of the values arising from the temporary presence of foreign thinkers and writers. Consideration of this matter might make it practicable for immigration laws to place temporary visitors in a separate category from permanent settlers, and subject these visitors only to such statutory and administrative restrictions upon freedom of thought and expression as may be desirable to protect the nation from the kinds of harms which might come from their temporary residence within its territory.

The McCarran Act, of course, is progress backward. It was easier for Marco Polo to go from Venice to the palace of Kublai Khan than it would be today for a repentant Venetian Fascist writer to go to an American University to deliver a lecture.

Finally, most of the Act is the old Mundt-Nixon Bill. It has very complicated provisions for the compulsory registration of every "Communist political organization" and every "Communist-front organization." The scheme is to be administered by a Subversive Activities Control Board, comprising five members appointed by the President and confirmed by the Senate, and serving for staggered terms of three years. Not more than three members shall belong to the same political party. The Board will have the power to classify any organization as either Communist-political or Communist-front and then order it to register. The Attorney General is to keep open to public inspection the registers of both types of organizations and the annual reports of the officers, finances, etc., which they are compelled to file. Every day of failure to register and every false statement or willful misleading omission in a registration statement or annual report is a separate offense on the part of the organization and individual officers.

The law provides for judicial review for Board decisions, but, in practice, this is not likely to be important. "The findings of the Board as to the facts, if supported by the preponderance of the evidence, shall be conclusive." Though the reviewing court may order additional evidence to be taken before the Board, it has no power itself to receive any new evidence. And any lawyer knows that the way in which testimony shapes up depends considerably upon the competence, experience, and fairness of the persons presiding at the actual trail. Moreover, the definitions in the law are so broad that it will be hard for judges to upset the Board's classification. Therefore, the operation of this law depends very largely on the five persons composing the Subversive Activities Control Board.

The present discussion will be confined to the provisions relating to "Communist-front organizations." Inasmuch as these provisions are likely to reach many groups whose purposes are cultural as well as political and who are engaged in exchanging ideas rather than winning elections, the interference with the lives of private citizens is much more extensive than in the case of "Communist political organizations." For the most part, however, the Act treats both types of organization alike. The principal differences are that the members of "Communist-front organizations" need not be listed in registration statements and annual reports, are not made ineligible for appointive federal offices or obliged to disclose their membership in seeking any office, and are not denied passports.

Something might be said for a registration law requiring *all* groups which attempt to influence public opinion to disclose the pertinent facts about themselves. The harmfulness of nondisclosure is by no means confined to "Communist-front organizations." For instance, virulent anti-Semitic pamphlets falsely accusing long lists of decent citizens with being disloyal are often widely mailed by organizations with high-sounding names, which take care not to mention their authors or the men who put up the money. A broad statute to break through this vicious anonymity of defamers of every sort is recommended in the 1947 Report of the President's Committee on Civil Rights. On the other hand, there is room for serious doubts whether such a statute will be a desirable remedy for this evil; it is likely to be enforced inefficiently and to stifle more good views than bad views. At all events, if Congress thinks a compulsory law for propaganda is needed, then it is needed for all sides of political, racial, and religious controversies. Such a law should seek to force into broad daylight *all the enemies of democracy* and not just a particular portion of them as in this Act.

Leaving the lopsidedness of the Act for later attention, let us see what this part of the law actually does. It enables five government officials to pick out certain groups and classify them as "Communist-front organizations." They are then subjected to numerous burdens from which social and propagandist groups are normally free. They must register, file lists of officers, keep supervised records and accounts, file annual reports, etc., under very severe penalties. Supporters will not receive income-tax deductions for their contributions, and the organizations themselves will no longer be tax-exempt. Finally, they must label every publication and the outside envelopes of all mail as coming from a "Communist organization"; this novel stigma recalls the practice of medieval princes to require Jews to wear special marks on their coats. All this virtually outlaws whatever organizations the five officials object to. Even if they are able to survive, they will have lost most of their moderate members and be wholly in the hands of extremists who don't care. Thus, they will be rendered more harmful than before.

First, I should like to point out the great dangers of thus interfering by law with freedom of discussion through organizations. The Act proposes to twist out of all recognizable shape one of the leading traditions of American life: the possibility of freely forming associations for all sorts of purposes—religious, political, social, and economic.

If we look back over our national history, we see that many of the most significant political and social changes began with the efforts of some small informal group disliked by the ordinary run of citizens. The abolition of slavery grew out of Garrison's Anti-slavery Society and similar associations. The Nineteenth Amendment is the culmination of the activities of a few unpopular women in the middle of the last century. The popular election of Senators, the federal income tax, and several other reforms largely originated with the Grangers and the Populists. American political, social, and economic institutions have developed to a very large extent through the interaction of propagandist groups. The appearance of a group favoring one side of an issue often aroused a group of opponents, and the public profited from its opportunity to judge between the competing presentations of both sides of an important national problem. Freedom of speech under the First Amendment has always meant more than the liberty of an isolated individual to talk about his ideas or put them into print. From the very beginning, freedom of speech has involved the liberty of a number of individuals to associate themselves for the advocacy of a common purpose. Thus, freedom of speech and freedom of assembly fit into each other. They are both related to the possibility of petitioning

Congress and the state legislatures for redress of grievances, which is only part of the wider freedom to submit the views of the individual or the group to the people at large for judgment.

It may be argued, however, that the so-called "Communist-front organizations" present an entirely new problem because they have objectionable purposes and include objectionable persons in their membership. This brings me to my second point. It has always been true of a great many propagandist organizations that their purposes were denounced by numerous law-abiding citizens and that their memberships included some extremists whose actions or ideas were open to serious adverse criticism. The books are full of denunciations by prominent citizens of abolitionists, women suffragists, labor unions, Populists, etc., which would more than match anything which has been written about the Joint Anti-Fascist Refugee Committee or the National Lawyers Guild or any of the other contemporary organizations listed as subversive by the House Un-American Activities Committee and the California legislative committees.

The membership situation is much the same now as it has always been. Propagandist organizations are not likely to be made up of men and women with conventional ideas. The very nature of a propagandist organization is that it wants to change something; obviously, then, it is likely to be made up of the kind of people who do want change. Such people vary a good deal. The core of the propagandist organization often consists of those whom Woodrow Wilson described as "forward-looking men and women," who disagree with the complacency of the ordinary run of citizens about some issue but still are fairly moderate in the changes they desire and so do not seriously offend their neighbors. Yet these are rarely the only members of a propagandist organization; it is likely also to include what Theodore Roosevelt called "the lunatic fringe." The organizations opposed to slavery had members who urged violations of law, such as rescuing fugitive slaves and transporting them to Canada on the Underground Railway. Some of them even favored or participated in the attempt of John Brown to start a slave-rising in Virginia. Time and again the whole labor movement has been denounced as lawless because some unionists undoubtedly engaged in violence against their employers and nonunion workers. Saloons were smashed by some prohibitionists, like Carrie Nation. It is plain that there is nothing new in the adherence of extremists to organizations with desirable, or at least legitimate, purposes.

Hence, we should not be surprised or frightened if some contemporary organizations for upholding the rights of minorities attract some members who are more in sympathy with Communism than the rank and file of the organization like. It is equally possible that organizations for upholding free speech or a fair trial or other fundamental constitutional rights may attract extremists whose interest is not in constitutional rights but in getting a Communist off. In short, it is inevitable that the membership of organizations formed to bring about change should include some persons who want a great deal of change.

The supporters of this Act assume that the moderate members of an organization always have an obligation to oust the extremists or else resign themselves. But this is by no means plain. Throughout the history of this country, the propagandist organizations which I have been describing were engaged in a hard fight against determined opponents. Their chances of winning this fight would clearly have been weakened if they had also waged an internal war with their own extremists or if moderates had got out and stopped supporting the cherished purpose of the organization. The practical question must have arisen hundreds of times: Was it better to put up with the extremists and continue the fight for an important cause, or disrupt the organization and probably kill the cause?

Now what would have happened in the history of our country if the policy of the McCarran Act had been embodied in law during the nineteenth century? There would have been different tests, of course, aimed at the kind of organization whose purpose was hated by the authorities of the particular period. Yet the general principle would have been exactly the same. The idea is to condemn an organization because of the objectionable ideas or conduct of its extremists and thus make it difficult for the moderates in the organization to accomplish their basic purpose. For example, suppose that the standards of permissible membership in antislavery societies had been fixed by a board chosen by slave owners and the owners of northern cotton mills. Again, suppose that the associations of employers and their friends in Congress had been able to set up a board to outlaw a trade union affiliated with men devoted to industrial violence.

When the membership and policies of an opinion-forming organization can be judged and controlled by outsiders with governmental power, all sorts of opportunities for the suppression of legitimate ideas arise. The officials, being outsiders, may be rather unsympathetic with the legitimate purposes of the organization. There is a tremendous temptation to opponents of those legitimate purposes to influence the selection and the behavior of the controlling officials. The presence of extremists can easily be made an excuse for outlawing an organization when *the real reason for getting rid of it is not fear of the extremists but hatred of the legitimate purposes.* The organization is suppressed, not because it might promote a revolution but because it might win elections and produce legislation.

There are many important public questions to be settled in this country today, on which much can be said on both sides. For example: Should we (a) oppose the totalitarian regime in Spain, or (b) resume normal diplomatic and commercial relations with Spain? Should we (a) give some measure of legal recognition to the present government of China, or (b) continue to supply billions of dollars to Chiang Kai-shek? Should we (a) decrease financial and military aid to Western Europe, or (b) continue or increase such aid? Should we (a) refuse to arm Western Germans for fear of a revival of the Nazis, or (b) arm them as a bulwark against the Soviet Union? These are vital questions, on which honest and reasonable men differ. They cannot be wisely decided unless individuals and opinion-forming organizations on the one side are as free to present their views as are those on the other side.

The significant thing is that in every one of these questions an organization which takes the (b) side cannot possibly be touched by the law, while any organization which takes the (a) side can conceivably be outlawed. Although there are plenty of honest reasons why many patriotic American citizens stand for the (a) side, it happens in every case that this side coincides with the views of the Soviet Union and its supporters, whose reasons are quite different. One of the factors which the Subversive Activites Control Board can take into consideration in determining whether an organization is "Communist-front" is "the extent to which the positions taken

. . . by it . . . on matters of policy do not deviate from those of any . . . Communist foreign government." Thus, this act leaves organizations on the (b) side untouched, no matter if they include Fascists, anti-Semites, and advocates of religious and racial hatred, and also greatly aids them by silencing a large number of their most vigorous opponents. Insofar as there are errors on the (b) side, the law will be increasing public danger enormously by making it very difficult for those errors to be combated by reason.

Actual experience amply justifies the expectation that the vague characterization of "Communist-front organizations" in this law will be used to outlaw or suppress many organizations which serve very desirable purposes, even if they do include some leftist people among their supporters. Remember always that everything depends on the five men who make up the Subversive Activities Control Board. The lopsided character of the determinations that may be expected is shown by the California list, which includes organizations opposing totalitarianism in Spain but none of those upholding it, many organizations favoring peace but none of those urging a devastating war, several organizations on behalf of Negroes but none of those upholding white supremacy. Its bias on purely domestic issues is shown by its including committees for freeing Tom Mooney, who was freed by the Governor of California; a committee for the defense of prisoners, who are guaranteed "the Assistance of Council" by the Sixth Amendment to our Constitution; and a committee to abolish the poll tax, which is surely a subject for legitimate political activity.

The reasoning by which many of these and other organizations are condemned consists of heaping one dubious inference on another dubious inference. An individual, *A*, is condemned because he belongs to X organization. Then the Y organization is condemned because it includes A. Then B is condemned because he belongs to the same organization as A. That brings down the Z organization, to which B also belongs. Since C, a fellow member of B in Z, is also a member of the X organization, that proves that X is subversive and we are right back where we started with no real evidence at any stage of the argument. When you discover that A and B are men like Professor Charles A. Beard and Senator Frank P. Graham of North Carolina, the absurdity of this whole process ought to be manifest.

Anything can happen when people get started on this business of outlawing groups, not for any crimes committed by either the group or any of its members, but for having some vaguely bad ideas or some vaguely bad members. Judge Dorothy Kenyon and Ambassador Philip Jessup are denounced to a Senate committee for belonging to various "subversive organizations" such as the Institute of Pacific Relations. When it is pointed out that this Institute included many persons of the highest reputation, the reply is made that any organization can attract some good members. Yet the attackers insist on judging both the Institute and Mr. Jessup by the supposed bad members and not by the admittedly good members. The whole business is based on the maxim, "Give a dog a bad name and hang him."

This statute creates a tremendous risk of outlawing a considerable number of groups of law-abiding people with inquiring minds, engaged in furthering some end which they believe to be in the very best interests of the United States. And, on the other hand, this law will encourage those who hate the patriotic purposes of such groups to do all they can to suppress them by influencing the selections of the five officials on the control board and by bringing pressure of every sort upon those officials. Instead of an orderly and enlightened search for the truth and wise policy, public opinion will be formed by coercion and intrigue. This law establishes government by misrepresentation.

Such are the bad effects of which the registration provisions are capable. No harm has been done as yet, because the Senate is still hesitating to confirm the President's nominees for the control board. His choices seem good men who will be forced to administer a bad act. The Senate's request for the files of the Federal Bureau of Investigation on these five men is indeed sinister. A nation has indeed gone far away from the ideals of the Philadelphia Convention of 1787 when the loyalty of its President is so distrusted by its legislature that the elected representatives of the people get guidance from the secret police.

In such a pass, what can calm patriots do? I see little hope for an early repeal of the McCarran Act, but we can hold up the hands of the President, Mr. McGrath, and the control board if they administer the registration provisions with a wise discretion, so as to interfere as little as its terms permit with the free flow of thought. Finally, I cannot repeat too often that everything depends on the individuals just mentioned and their successors. If this Act remains law in January 1953, and if the Republican Party is then largely directed by Senator McCarran and Senator McCarthy, a change of administration will make this one of the most evil laws ever enacted by the Congress of the United States. Imagine what Thomas Jefferson would say of this tyranny over the mind of man. As Alan Barth says, "Nothing that the agents of Communism have done or can do in this country is so dangerous to the United States as what they have induced us to do to ourselves."

* * *

The real enemies of mankind are not in some special region of earth but in the conditions all men face—famine, disease, ignorance, injustice, greed, cruelty, abuse of power, and mental unbalance. The dark places of the mind are nearer than we think. Hitler and his associates are only one example of this. There is the terrifying danger that political and social organization and human understanding cannot develop fast enough to cope with the advance of science and invention.

To preserve the integrity and dignity of the individual human being through ever-increasing complexities is a baffling task. Yet it is our task. As Du Pont de Nemours wrote from France to Jefferson: "We are only snails with the peaks of the Andes to climb. By God, we must climb!"

Walter Gellhorn

SECURITY, SECRECY, AND
THE ADVANCEMENT OF SCIENCE

MODERN man well recognizes the centrally important role
of science in his life. Whether one be most concerned with
health or with crops or with industrial productivity, one's
well-being is largely affected by the scientist's work. And if
one happens to be most concerned with national power in
an era of international tension, one knows again that the
scientist is close to the core of the problem, for national
power is in the end merely the sum of the health and the
crops and the industrial productivity of individuals.

That is why, in this age of crises, so much of our country's
wealth is devoted to scientific pursuits and to the development of the scholar's researches. Secrecy does not hide the
extent of our commitments. The nuclear fission experiments
that were launched so quietly in academic laboratories at
Columbia and Chicago led first to a small atomic furnace
built unobtrusively beneath the unused football stands of the
University of Chicago. Today the Atomic Energy Commission's installations and grounds cover more area than the
states of Delaware and Rhode Island combined. A new
diffusion plant near Paducah will alone consume almost as
much electricity as the entire city of Chicago. The Savannah

River project for tritium-plutonium production is just now commencing in a modest way by biting 250,000 acres out of South Carolina's farmland, sweeping villages and homes before it.

Developments like these are new and they are dramatic. Their drama and novelty must not obscure the fact, however, that they are far from unique. Well over fifty per cent of all the scientific research done in America today is supported by federal funds—more than a billion dollars annually for agronomical, astronomical, and aeronautical research; biological, ballistical, and bacterial research; animal, vegetable, and mineral research; civilian, military, and nondescript research. The armed forces alone have placed some 20,000 contracts calling for investigations or development in institutional and industrial laboratories across America, while the government's own research centers (the military services have over fifty such installations, with 50,000 employees, and various civilian agencies have numerous separate research establishments) are crowded with yet other projects. If not a single penny were being spent on atomic and hydrogen bombs, the demands of military science would surely be no less clamorous but would merely press in some slightly different direction. Though our economy may strain and groan under martial pressures, we are nevertheless not likely to abandon the scientific projects that are giant consumers of physical and human resources.

Partly because the undertakings of today are so inhumanly massive, Americans sometimes behave as though Science were a depersonalized reality. It is allowed to become a tag term that, like Capital or Labor or Religion or Politics, suggests an independent entity beyond human governance. But of course Science is human knowing and human finding out. It is the observations of men and women, their speculation, their skilled resourcefulness. We cannot discuss the problems of national security in the realm of science except by discussing human beings.

*   *   *

The tradition of scientists has been publication. The achievements of one, reported by word or by writing, have been the foundation bricks used by another in the never-ending building up of understanding. "The cumulative nature of scientific knowledge," says Nobel Laureate I. I. Rabi, "puts the scientist in such great debt to the past and to his contemporary colleagues that his responsibility to present his results can hardly be honorably evaded."

Today, in large sections of science, it is no longer possible to discharge that great debt in the traditional way. By law and by military regulation scientists are forbidden to communicate their findings, nor may they discuss their perplexities with others who could perhaps aid in overcoming them. The purpose is obvious. We wish not to equip potential enemies with insights that could lead to weapons that might be turned against us. And so we restrain the circulation of scientific intelligence that might further researches elsewhere.

By and large the restrictions on interchange of knowledge are well related to their declared justification. Decision as to what must be kept secret has for the most part in recent years been left to trained scientists rather than to military zealots. Even so, there is always a pressure toward blocking rather than opening the channels of discussion. Officials whose discretion will determine whether or not there shall be publication have little to fear from over-strictness. Criticism or court martial may follow a release from secrecy restrictions, but not from their imposition. Thus, for a long time after the French had undoubtedly duplicated our early reactor successes and for many months after the Russians had produced an atomic explosion, the Atomic Energy Commission still hesitated to abate the secrecy that obscured primitive and now wholly obsolete American work in the nuclear energy field. This was not because national security was served by keeping American researchers in ignorance of "secrets" that were already so widely shared abroad. It was because the AEC was cowed by Congressional and journalistic critics who have regarded common sense as a betrayal of the nation's interests.

Professor Robert F. Bacher, a former AEC Commissioner, acknowledges (as do we all) that legitimate restrictions rest on information about weapons design and production. "But," he adds, "the veil of secrecy has a tendency to spread like a fog and cover all sorts of other subjects as well. No one wants to be responsible for making information generally available which someone might claim should remain secret. As a result, many developments are kept secret which might have led to major advances elsewhere in American industry." Many a nuclear scientist says, only half jokingly, that the surest way to retard Russian work would be to ship to the appropriate commissariat the boxcar of blueprints relating to our first atomic energy endeavors. While the Russians were occupying themselves with deciphering and applying our outmoded specifications, we could forge far ahead, achieving security by progress rather than by secrecy. But desecretizing, no matter how advantageous it might be, is unlikely to occur so long as the AEC is subjected to denunciation (as it has been) for disclosing the important "secret" that a smoke stack at Brookhaven National Laboratory rises 420 feet in the air and can be seen from afar.

In any event, the real area of scientific secrecy is not measurable in terms of specific prohibitions. Professor Samuel K. Allison, who was director during the war of the Metallurgical Laboratory, at the heart of our atomic energy project, puts it this way: "The existence of an inner core of secret facts vitiates whole areas of scientific inquiry and technological development extending far from the actually classified data. No one can remember from day to day just what is classified, and to be safe, avoids discussing whole fields of research and technology."

Almost with a single voice American scientists assert that we are overdoing our secrecy. Unless we regard them as fools or scoundrels, we should perhaps devote some pretty sober thought to their views:

American scientists say that the effort to keep secrets is over-costly when long continued;

American scientists say that retardation of our own scientific work is the price of retarding others; and since we have superior reserves of trained manpower and of material resources, we tend to immobilize ourselves in the aggregate even more than we immobilize our competitors;

American scientists say that when new findings are placed under a blanket, we lose the chance of utilizing them in unsuspected ways; scientific progress has been chiefly characterized by the unpredictable adaptations of learning—as, for example, when Roentgen's discovery of X-rays led in time to recognition of the electron and thus to a great new technology;

American scientists say that erection of artificial barriers between scientific workers makes for duplication of effort, for loss of stimulus through criticism and shared ideas, and for the growth of castes outside the great confraternity of science;

American scientists say, too, that the training of new men—the ones who will have to lead in the developments of five or ten or fifteen years from now—becomes increasingly difficult and in some fields quite impossible.

"At present," declares Philip Morse, a distinguished physicist who has moved from M.I.T. to the Department of Defense, "no adequate course in nuclear engineering can be taught at a university; the material is too secret." The same weight of secrecy prevents instruction in many other subjects of vital importance to the nation, so that the pinch of personnel shortages may in time prevent our achieving the achievable. Just recently it was necessary to shut down important nuclear energy developmental work because hydrogen bomb problems demanded the services of the too few available scientists. It is worth recalling that there are now employed in Atomic Energy Commission work alone as many physicists as there were in the whole of the United States in 1920. The nation lacks the scientific manpower it can so readily use, not only for the elaboration of military destructiveness but for the continuation of life enrichment. But the nation, despite its lack, still hesitates. Its hesitation means that the oncoming generation can not readily equip itself for fresh endeavors in science.

In so complex a matter a dogmatic conclusion would be unseemly. Still, there is perhaps room for a tentative judgment. Obviously no one wishes to jeopardize national safety by incautious disclosure of military secrets. That does not mean, however, that national safety will be enhanced by an enforced return to the Dark Ages through suppressing all scientific information. Even though bits and pieces of knowledge may be added together in terrifying ways, we all recognize that retreat into impenetrable ignorance is scarcely the road to strength. So a line must be marked between the ideas that should be published for mankind's benefit and, on the other side, the military researches that ought to remain bottled up for self-preservation.

No doubt the boundaric cannot be rigidly drawn; the ebb and flow of international tension will be reflected in the slackness or tautness of the dividing line. In general, however, normal human exchange of information ought to be forestalled only when the information in question is solely of military significance. Weapons design, performance and production records, specifications of processes and instrumentation are matters that can be locked away without gravely jeopardizing the advance of science or civilian industry. But if military significance were alone to be the determinant of secrecy, the consequences would be boundless.

Almost all matters of science and technology are likely to have military value in some degree. A sure cure for the common cold, as an example, would immeasurably improve the efficiency of any army. Should its discovery therefore be a military secret? Some military authorities believe that it should be. During the last war we carefully restricted publication of new light on typhus, apparently because exposure of enemy troops to this ancient scourge might be a military advantage for our side; of course disease-bearing lice make no nice distinctions between men in uniform and refugees in rags, so our secrecy had other than military consequences. Even today we scrupulously conceal the fruits of research in our biological warfare project. An official report reveals that there has been discovery of "methods for the rapid and accurate detection of minute quantities of disease-producing agents"; but these methods have not been disclosed to the epidemiologists and others who are more concerned with life than with death.

Surely it must be possible to discern a difference between matters that deal with human needs and matters that deal only with war. Even the totality of modern warfare need not blind us to the fact that ignorance is the primary enemy of all mankind, ourselves as well as the nation's potential enemies. A purely hypothetical military advantage in an international contest that may not soon (perhaps not ever) occur cannot justify restraints upon knowledge that will aid in the ever-present war against ignorance.

* * *

"Secrecy and progress are incompatible. This is always true of science, whether for military purposes or otherwise. Science flourishes and scientists make progress in an atmosphere of free inquiry and free interchange of ideas, with the continual mutual stimulation of active minds working in the same or related fields. Any imposition of secrecy in science is like application of a brake to progress." These are not the words of a dweller in an academic ivory tower. They are the words of Karl T. Compton, then chairman of the Research and Development Board of the National Military Establishment.

"It is much easier for the average citizen to understand secrecy," Compton went on to say, "than it is for him to understand the conditions necessary for scientific progress. I am sure that the pendulum has recently swung so far in the direction of concern over secrecy regarding even little details and unimportant people that our real security is suffering. It is suffering from the slowing up of progress because attention is being diverted from the really big things which need to be done."

Every observation confirms Dr. Compton's statement. The more we broaden the area of scientific secrecy, the more morbidly consuming becomes our preoccupation with conserving the "secrets" we already have and the more cumbersome becomes our effort to acquire more. This is manifested, among other ways, by extreme caution in granting permission to persons to work within the guarded zones.

The world being what it is, no one can quarrel with the use of preventive measures against faithlessness and corruption. The personnel security programs that are administered by the Atomic Energy Commission and the military services have as their goals the forestalling of sabotage, espionage, and pure irresponsibility. Those are goals that command support. If one quarrels with the programs, it is not because of their purposes but because of their effects.

Here is how the process works in the AEC. Scientific and technical data about nuclear fission are declared by law to be secret—or, in the technical word, "restricted"—unless and until the AEC says otherwise. No individual may have access to restricted data "until the Federal Bureau of Investigation shall have made an investigation and report to the Commission on the character, associations and loyalty of such individual and the Commission shall have determined that permitting such person to have access to restricted data will not endanger the common defense or security."

The power and duty to pass on the "character, associations and loyalty" of scientists is thus not limited to those who work for the AEC itself, nor even to those who work for the larger contractors like General Electric or Du Pont or Carbide & Carbon that operate the major AEC installations. "Clearance" is a necessity as well for every academic or industrial researcher whose scientific work involves a scrap of "restricted data."

By the end of 1950 more than 200,000 persons (of course,

not all of them scientists or technicians) had been investigated and had been given by the AEC access to restricted information or to restricted areas. Half of the Commission's meetings and a third of its meeting-time were devoted to personnel security matters. Two thousand three hundred cases were held for further review to determine whether clearance should be granted. About 700 were finally cleared after further investigation. The other 1,600 resigned or were denied clearance.

Interestingly enough, the "derogatory information" about scientific workers that has turned up in AEC cases has infrequently reflected misconduct or serious questions about character. Almost all the cases have involved supposed ideas or associations—a man's mother-in-law is reported to be a "Red," or his sister contributed to the Joint Anti-Fascist Refugee Committee, or he had once attended a summer camp that was run by a coöperative society, or he has played in a string quartet with another scientist who later came under official suspicion. Applicants have rarely been challenged because they were found to be wicked men. When clearance has been denied, it has been because of a fear that someone or other *might* be wicked at some future time, usually because he knows someone else who might be wicked or because he has voiced a "radical" opinion.

The process is well-meaning but inefficient. No doubt the Soviet Union utilizes the services of espionage agents in this country, just as this country does abroad. No doubt some of its agents are scientifically trained. But an ideas-and-associations test will rarely unmask them. The chemist Harry Gold, who never worked for the government but who acted as conduit between the British physicist Fuchs and his Soviet contacts, described his career in these terms: "I was told by my superior to stay away from the Communist Party, never to read the *Daily Worker*, and never to read liberal literature or express liberal thoughts." More often than not, one may assume, the men who are real security risks will avoid wearing lapel buttons that attract attention to them. During all the years of tension between the U.S.S.R. and this country since World War II, not a single scientist involved in American security clearance proceedings has been found to be either a professional or amateur spy, tool, or pipeline. While the "loyalty" of scientists as a group has been called into question by some of our more exclamatory Congressional figures, there have been no revealed instances of faithlessness in this country that would support what former Commissioner W. W. Waymack calls "the periodic hubbubs."

Meanwhile, however, both the AEC and the armed forces play a pretty rough game with scientists whose unconventionality is equated with untrustworthiness. The figures of rejections do not tell the whole story. In addition to those who are held up for inquiry, there are large numbers who simply refuse to apply for clearance because they fear indignities.

It may be guessed that the very men who launched our atomic energy program in the first place, men like Einstein and Szilard and Urey and Fermi, might have clearance difficulties today if to them were applied the same tests that must be faced by lesser known figures; for these great scientists have sinned by freely expressing critical opinions or by having kinsmen in distant places. The chief of our microwave radar work during the war recently wrote that if post-war conditions had obtained when he was recruiting his scientific staff, many of those who largely contributed to our success would never have had a chance to participate in the war effort. Moreover, he added, the response of others would not have been so generous.

The discomforting delays and uncertainties of clearance procedure deter many sober, reliable, unchallengeable scientists from entering secret laboratories. Each time that word of a "clearance difficulty" passes through the channels of professional gossip, there is a sort of collective shudder. When it is known that a man's clearance was held up because in his youth he had joined the United People's Action Committee for the announced purpose of combating racial discrimination in Philadelphia, some other potential recruit—recalling his own indiscretions or enthusiasms—decides not to expose his valuable reputation to a like hazard. Or, if he himself is already cleared, he may think twice before suggesting the appointment of a fellow-scientist who is regarded as a "liberal." Partly this is to save a friend from possible embarrassment. Partly it is to save his own reputation, for if those with whom he is "sympathetically associated" fail to gain security clearance, of course his own standing is affected.

Timidity is thus dually inspired. And timidity drastically narrows the ranks of those who may be deemed eligible. One of America's most distinguished physiologists was recently proposed, without his knowledge or initiative, for an important post. Before decision was finally made, his name was withdrawn from consideration because it was thought—quite mistakenly, as a matter of fact—that he had been a Progressive Party supporter in 1948. There was no question of clearance denial, because there was never any formal request for clearance. An honest though erroneous belief about a fact that was in any event very probably immaterial operated as a fully effective barrier. It is this sort of thing that hides beneath the statistics. Ebullience of the spirit is not a quality in large demand when orthodoxy is the only sure guarantor of clearance.

Do the crudities of personnel security measures suggest that they should be abandoned altogether? Of course not. Just as secrecy is in some aspects warranted because it may impede the military progress of those we distrust, so too are personnel security programs justified as guards against infidelity. When they are irrationally extended, however, both sorts of protective measures may defeat us instead of our enemies. Neither step is desirable as an end in itself. Each has its grave costs. They are worth while only when the danger that would flow from disclosure is real rather than the product of strained imagining.

In the end we shall be better off if we can compress the area of secrecy, and if we can recognize that intellectual diversity has little to do with suitability for national service.

* * *

Wholly apart from the literally tens of thousands of scientific workers who must be cleared because they work in "sensitive areas" there are some thirty thousand federal employees who have professional ratings as geologists, bacteriologists, physicists, pathologists, entomologists, and so on. Still other thousands are professionally trained—for example, the doctors and dentists and psychologists of the Veterans Administration, the officers of the Public Health Service, and the medical corps of the Bureau of Indian Affairs. Few of these men and women deal with restricted data; and whenever they do touch the concerns of the military or the AEC, they must obtain security clearance in the same way as persons outside the government. No secrets, scientific or

otherwise, normally attach to their work. They are engaged
in research on tuberculosis and on the Japanese beetle, rather
than on germ warfare and submarines. They administer Was-
sermann and Rorschach tests rather than tests of new atomic
weapons. The diseases of poultry and swine and man, the
problems of foresters and fishermen and miners, the stars and
the earth's depths—these are their provinces. The shaping of
international policies, the creation or the unraveling of military mysteries do not fall to them. Yet the associations and
the politics of these federal scientists undergo the most
scrupulous examination as though the nation's safety were
at stake.

This is the product of Executive Order No. 9835, the so-
called Loyalty Order, promulgated by President Truman on
March 21, 1947, to afford the United States "maximum protection . . . against infiltration of disloyal persons into the
ranks of its employees." Every employee or would-be employee of any "non-sensitive" federal agency must now, as
is well known, be investigated by the FBI and must be
excluded if "reasonable grounds exist for belief that the
person involved is disloyal to the Government of the United
States." The initial determination as to the existence of
"reasonable grounds" is made by loyalty boards established
for that purpose, the power of ultimate review being lodged
in a Loyalty Review Board appointed by the President.

The critical issue in any program of this sort is whether
disloyalty is to be evidenced by deeds or whether, instead,
it is regarded as a state of mind that can be discovered
through the individual's opinions and contacts. The latter
is the view now in favor.

The Loyalty Order adds nothing whatever to the government's power to discharge or discipline employees who are

suspected of actual misconduct. Nor does the Loyalty Order generate the authority to oust Communists from the federal service. Ever since the Hatch Act of 1939 there has been a prohibition of the employment of anyone who belongs to "any political party or organization which advocates the overthrow of our constitutional form of government"; and the Attorney General has long since ruled that this requires instant removal of Communists. The novelty of the Loyalty Order lies in its provision that a person may be dismissed because of "Membership in, affiliation with or sympathetic association with any foreign or domestic organization, association, movement, group or combination of persons designated by the Attorney General as totalitarian, fascist, communist, or subversive . . ." This, indeed, is the very heart of the whole program, for most of the charges have been brought under this single section.

The "black list" compiled by the Attorney General now places six organizations in the "subversive" category. Of these only three are extant—the Communist Party and two anti-Stalinist but actively Marxist groups of lesser size. A much larger number have been characterized as "communist." These are the so-called "front" organizations. By definition they have open and lawful purposes that may attract the support of non-communist individuals. But their characteristic seems to be that Communists are influential in them or are active in their management; and since Communists presumably never waste their time, this suggests that the motives and goals of the organizations are not solely the ones that appear on the surface. In any event, whatever may be the tests applied by the Attorney General (and they have never been revealed), once he has privately completed his labeling process the matter is closed. An individual charged with sympathy for an organization cannot challenge the Attorney General's conclusion; nor can the organization itself; nor, of course, can a loyalty board inquire into the issue on its own motion.

No one in a position of authority has ever suggested that mere membership in or sympathetic association with a blacklisted organization constitutes absolute proof of disloyalty. It is merely evidence to be weighed along with everything else that is pertinent. In fact, however, this is the bit of evidence that sets in motion the whole course of investigation and inquisition that leads to a final conclusion.

A federal employee today may face charges of disloyalty based on long past and sometimes almost forgotten contacts with groups or individuals. Even groups that have not been stigmatized by the Attorney General but have been denounced by the less restrained members of the House Committee on Un-American Activities, may prove to be major embarrassments. Personal associations—as, for example, between parent and child, husband and wife, or college classmates—have given rise to the dismaying assertion that there is reasonable ground for doubting a man's loyalty to his country. The expression of the traditional view that even Communists are entitled, under our constitution, to a protection of their civil liberties, has been made the basis for the same terrible accusation. In one case an employee who had long served the government was placed under charges because unidentified informants asserted that he had "advocated the Communist Party line, *such as favoring peace and civil liberties*" and that his "convictions concerning equal rights for all races and classes extend slightly beyond the normal feelings of the average individual."

Are charges like these the normality of the loyalty program? I would hesitate to say that they are. On the whole the program has been administered with moderation and good sense. Nevertheless cases like the ones just suggested are not at all aberrational. They reflect the insistence of the Loyalty Review Board that charges be issued and cases taken to hearing whenever the files contain so-called "derogatory information" that has not been wholly explained away. Since information is deemed to be derogatory if it even tenuously ties a federal employee to a suspect individual or blacklisted organization, many cases reach the final stages of indignity, though without any serious belief in official quarters that the employee will be found disloyal. Consequently, most of the cases—some six out of seven—that go to hearing end in acquittals. Meanwhile, however, a federal employee has been put to the expense of a trial, and, what is much more important, to the shame and terror aroused by the shattering charge of disloyalty.

Many thoroughly decent people regard this as merely an unfortunate cost of a necessary protective measure. I cannot agree. The unintentional destruction of civil servants is not a needed element of any proper public program, nor does it enlarge by the slightest degree the margin of our national safety. On the contrary it depresses the morale of those all too few public employees who are live-spirited and accustomed to independent thought.

The nation's leading scientists have warned time and time again that the miasma of suspicion that envelops government service today, hovering with special thickness around brain-workers, has deterred scientists from entering or remaining in public employment. As to those who do remain, there is a special factor that may lessen their professional as well as their personal vigor. Cases are well known in which a federal scientist has had to account for his knowing or corresponding with a fellow scientist whose politics were not regarded as irreproachable. This discourages professional relationships and the stimulus that comes from exchanged ideas; for unless one is prepared to precede his scientific inquiries by an inquiry into a new acquaintance's political orientation, one may later have to apologize for his incaution.

We have been quick to recognize in other countries the vicious absurdity of identifying scientific reliability with absolute political conformity. We have been able to see, in retrospect, that many of the Nazis' scientific failures were attributable to the stupidities of their personnel policies. We see today, in the Soviet Union and in some of its satellite countries, the witless degradation of scientists whose theories fail to support the dogmas of the ruling force. What we have still to see is that our own loyalty program may itself be a step on the same tragic road that others have trod. The action taken under that program for nearly four years has rarely dealt with any objectionable behavior of federal scientists and other federal employees. It has dealt with the supposed content of their minds and emotions. The insecurity engendered by fear can, like a disease, paralyze the creativity of those whose whole careers may be spoiled by charges. If that should be a consequence of the loyalty program in the United States, this country will indeed have paid heavily for it.

For what? What, precisely, has the program accomplished? Clearly it has not brought repose to federal employees, for no one knows today what professional or nonprofessional opinions may arouse suspicion against him; nor can one, once given the stamp of approval, be sure that political blasting will not reopen his case. Clearly the program has not convinced the American people that they are well served by loyal employees; widespread suspicion underlies the alarmingly ready response to the blackguarding tactics that have most recently been dubbed "McCarthyism." Clearly the operation has not laid bare an infection in the body politic; those who administer the program have publicly announced that "not one single case of espionage" has been brought to light, and have said that the FBI in all its thousands of investigations has found no evidence even "directing toward espionage."

What, then, has the program achieved? In my judgment it has achieved one major result, and that a bad one. It has thrown the weight of the government of the United States behind the dangerous theory that entertaining an unsound opinion or advocating an abhorrent idea is in itself an offense against society. Acceptance of that theory discourages bold speculation by making it dangerous to dissent, for in nervous times dissent is too readily mistaken for disaffection. When diversity of opinion becomes personally disastrous, most people simply avoid peril by suddenly avoiding opinions. The national administration lost its chance to resist those who pretend that every nonconformist is the likely tool of international conspirators. Instead, through its loyalty program, it lent respectability to the lamentable tendency to denounce rather than merely disagree. This is the chief, the bitter fruit of nation-wide inquisitions into what a man is thinking and into whom he knows and into what he reads, instead of into his behavior.

In statistical terms the loyalty program is unimpressive. Some 3,000,000 federal employees have been scrutinized. About 300 of this number were discharged on findings of potential disloyalty—approximately one ten-thousandth of those involved. While investigations were in progress another group of employees—something less than 3,000—terminated their service; some of these probably left because they feared the expense or the outcome of loyalty proceedings, but the total includes those who died, retired, or resigned for wholly unrelated causes. In any event, unless it is thought that the FBI and the loyalty boards have been wretchedly derelict in their assigned duties, these figures suggest how infrequent is the incidence of disloyalty in the federal service, even under the artificially enlarged tests that the Loyalty Order legitimatized.

The program should be abandoned as a mistaken approach to a real problem.

To whatever extent may be truly required by security considerations, that is, in "sensitive" positions wherever they may occur in the federal service, we should insist that jobholders have the fullest confidence of their superiors. When an employee is reasonably thought to be a "security risk" in a sensitive job, let him be moved at once to a nonsensitive post if possible and if no misconduct on his part has been involved.

As for employees already in nonsensitive areas—the men who are engaged in cardiac research or in efforts to preserve the whooping crane from extinction or in the synthesis of cortisone—reliance should be placed on administration rather than detection. Without doubt the government should dismiss such a man if he is disloyal to his job, whatever be his motivation. That sort of disloyalty, however, is within the province of supervisory officials rather than FBI agents.

To detect disloyalty involving criminality or reflecting a duality of national allegiance, we must rely on the highly effective counter-espionage work of federal investigators; the record till today shows us that what spies and saboteurs there may be are not likely to be caught in the coarse meshes of loyalty probes, even when the probers are from the FBI. And as for the "disloyalty" that is now thought to be reflected in affiliations or associations that are entirely within the law, the best thing for us to do is to laugh at them. The nation's safety will be enhanced rather than lessened by freeing the FBI from the preoccupation with picayune things that the loyalty program has forced upon it.

*   *   *

This country's personnel and secrecy policies were not ignobly framed. On the contrary, they were laid down by men who were sincerely and patriotically convinced of their necessity. Moreover, they have been administered on the whole moderately, though sometimes without the subtle sophistication that might have prevented damaging follies.

Nonetheless they have in part responded to and in part themselves set in motion an unfortunate current in American life. We come at times dangerously close to discarding our own best traditions. In America's history, change has not been thought subversive, except in the sense that the plow subverts the soil. Belief that our country has not yet achieved perfection has not suggested disloyalty; on the contrary, a man's devotion has been measurable by the zeal with which he sought to improve what already he loved. There have always been Americans who preferred to swim in swiftly flowing streams rather than in still pools; and while the wisdom of the preference might often be debated, the underlying motive was rarely questioned. Today the suspicions distilled from fear and hate threaten to change our tolerance of diversity and to drive us toward an enforced similarity erroneously described as unity.

This cannot be justified in the name of national security. As Alan Barth has well reminded, "The function of national security in a totalitarian society is to preserve the State, while the function of national security in a free society is to preserve freedom." Freedom, therefore, must be the dominant goal of the measures we employ. We cannot afford to be diverted from it by some scrap of short-range expediency, nor can we accept it as a somewhat dubious luxury to be enjoyed only when the times are placid and tempers are good. Like an unused muscle, freedom when not exercised tends to waste away.

The struggle for men's hearts and minds is not solely a struggle between the United States and the Soviet Union. In a real sense the struggle is taking place here at home, a wholly domestic contest. We Americans proclaim with pride our allegiance to the principles of freedom. Most of us are prepared to fight for freedom if need be. But we need more than instinctive readiness to fight. We need an aware belief, a passionate faith in the professed principles we are so prone to abandon in practice.

Fear has been guiding too many of the steps that have affected American scientists—the magnifying of the area in which restraints on interchange have slowed or prevented work; the readiness to denounce scientists individually and en masse, so that recruitment has become an increasingly urgent problem; the reliance upon associative tests and predictive findings of untrustworthiness to ward off the phantom of disloyalty. Fear is an immobilizer, not a stimulator. Fear is a destroyer, not a builder. If we wholly succumb to its promptings, we shall defeat our hope for solid achievement, for firm foundations in a long-continuing crisis. The answer to fear, as J. Robert Oppenheimer has well said, cannot always lie in dissipating its causes or in yielding to it. Sometimes it lies, simply enough, in courage.

Curtis Bok

CENSORSHIP AND THE ARTS

ℐ HAVE been assigned the task of talking about censorship as applied to the arts. This is such a large order that we must first decide what we are talking about. By censorship I mean the official suppression, restriction, or punishment of free expression.

Having said that, we can dispose briefly of all of history before the year 1501, when Pope Alexander VI, one of the most corrupt and worldly of the Popes in the bad days of the Church, established the principle of modern censorship by his bull prohibiting unlicensed printing. Before the invention of the printing press in about 1470, there was no method of multiplying books, plays, or pictures in such a way that they could affect the mass of the population. We hear of Plato paying the modern equivalent of $3,000 for three books by Philolaus. If books indirectly affected the general population by affecting the minds of its rulers and ruling class, the matter rested at that level and was not of direct public concern. Hence the suppression of those arts that now depend on printing was inconsiderable and was limited to incidents like Caligula's attempt to suppress Homer, and the Emperor Domitian's killing Hermogenes of

Tarsus because of passages in his history, and having the books of Junius Rusticus burned in the Forum.

Such incidents arose out of utterances considered too libelous, too treasonable, or too derogatory of the gods. None of them was the result of legislation, nor did any occur because of obscenity; even Ovid's exile to the desolate shores of the Euxine was less on account of his "Art of Love"—which is still a thorn in the flesh of United States postal inspectors—than because, possibly in trying to put his art into practice, Ovid insulted the Emperor's daughter.

The arts that were open to most people in the ancient world were sculpture and painting and, to some degree, the theatre. I have the impression that these forms of expression were quite free then and were bound by custom and not by law. There was a flurry in Greece at one time over naked statues, and the fig leaf made its appearance. It was also the custom that women did not attend the Greek theatre, which may account for the breadth of some of Aristophanes' comedies that caused Plutarch to call them coarse and vulgar: but *Lysistrata*, then as now, was performed quite openly. If an artist refrained from insulting the gods or the rulers too grossly, he had little to fear from anything except the wholesome grinders of public opinion. After all, if the Romans could feed people to the lions in public, they were not likely to be too squeamish in other directions. It is true, I believe, that no system of pre-publication licensing had ever been heard of before the sixteenth century.

With the breakdown of the Roman Empire into much smaller governmental units, with relatively weak monarchies and strong city states or feudal overlordships, the horizons of life shrank greatly. The communication of ideas and art forms had to depend largely on the minnesingers, the troubadours, and the Crusaders returning from the wars. The central vitality of civilization passed to the Church, which from the early days of its history was increasingly alert for heresy and perfected the weapon of the Inquisition as a defense. Life as a whole was naturally too narrow to make censorship as we know it necessary, except for the notion of heresy, and even heresy was only an exaggerated form of disobedience that was dealt with like any other disobedience—the victim was exiled, tortured, or simply put to death. We mustn't forget that until well within the past two hundred years the English Criminal Code punished 222 offenses with death.

Censorship as a conception did not arise until the flood of books from the newly invented presses presented a clear and present danger, which was aggravated by the threat of the Reformation to the preëminence of the Church. Almost a century before Caxton printed his first book in 1474, Pope Martin V threatened those who read heretical books with excommunication, because of the doctrines that Wyckliffe and Huss were preaching in the dawn of the theological revolution.

Following Alexander VI's bull in 1501, the rulers in France, Germany, and England made printing a monopoly by granting prerogatives to a few specific persons. For nearly two centuries there was no such thing as a free press in England, and infringement of the licensing laws was punished by cropping of the ears, slitting of the tongue, and hanging. After the abolition of the Star Chamber in 1641, Parliament took up the cudgels at about the time that a young man of thirty-five, named John Milton, took a month's vacation and to everyone's astonishment brought home with him a bride. Her name was Mary Powell, and she was a flighty young lady of seventeen, the daughter of an ardent Royalist. After living with the difficult John for a month, Mary went home to her parents and sent word to him that she would not return. Shortly afterward, Milton produced two powerful pieces on divorce, contending that the sacramental idea in marriage was a priestly superstition and that incompatibility was sufficient ground for divorce. The outcry was tremendous and took two forms: one, that the essays were immoral, and two, that they were illegal; as indeed they were, since Parliament had passed an ordinance on June 14, 1643, that no book might be published until it had first been approved by official censors and until the author and publisher had been registered with the Stationer's Company.

Milton had observed neither formality, and a proceeding against him in contempt came before both Houses in Parliament. Milton then leveled his big guns at the Lords and Commons, again without the formality of license or registration, and the result was the *Areopagitica,* which, while it did not immediately cause the repeal of the obnoxious Ordinance, delivered a virtual death-blow to the system of pre-publication licensing. No such system could stand against words like these:

And though all the winds of doctrine were let loose to play upon the earth, so Truth be in the field, we do injuriously by licensing and prohibiting to misdoubt her strength. Let her and Falsehood grapple: who ever knew Truth put to the worse, in a free and open encounter? . . . Give me the liberty to know, to utter, and to argue freely according to conscience, above all liberties.

The *Areopagitica* appeared on November 25, 1644. The Licensing Act did not expire finally until 1692, and the last restrictions on the English press were not removed until a court decision in 1765 and an Act of Parliament in 1775.

It is interesting to note that freedom of the press is not mentioned in the English Bill of Rights and hence has a constitutional rather than a legal foundation. It is also interesting that the earliest mandate for a free press appears in the first constitutions of Delaware, Maryland, North Carolina, and Pennsylvania, in 1776. In the United States the freedom of the press dates effectively from the now famous trial of John Peter Zenger, whom Andrew Hamilton, in 1735, persuaded a jury to acquit against all existing legal precedents, and in the teeth of a licensing law not unlike that of Milton's day.

      ✿   ✿   ✿

The focus of restriction on free expression remained upon heresy for about two hundred years after Milton. The first Index Librorum Prohibitorum of the Catholic Church appeared in 1559, and there is an edition of the *Decameron*, a most lusty book, that appears with the Papal Imprimatur, the heresy carefully removed but the obscenity untouched. With the separation of Church from State and the supremacy of the State established, the focus of censorship then turned to treason, where it remains now, or at least has been revived, in totalitarian countries. But another force was at work that caused it to turn again. The Renaissance lifted the lid from art generally, and the reaction to it, which we know as Victorianism, finally crystallized the idea of obscenity as being against the public interest. Obscenity then became the new point of focus.

As late as 1707 the English Law Courts said that there was no law to punish obscenity; it was a matter for the ecclesiastical authority. In 1727, however, the Law Lords reversed themselves, and obscenity for the first time became part of the English common law. There were few, if any, prosecutions for it until well into Victoria's reign, where things came to a head with Lord Campbell's Act. The cause for this legislation was the read-easies in Holyoke Street, where one could go and for a fee read one's choice of pornography. Public opinion, which had grown very moral by this time, discovered that while obscenity was indictable at common law, there was no legal provision for searching for and seizing the offensive material. Shopkeepers calculated a bit of time in jail as a business risk, leaving their wives to run the shop in their absence, and knowing, then as now, that arrests for violations of the moral laws are uneven and sporadic. Lord Campbell's Act supplied the necessary measures, but Parliament had a wretched time deciding what obscenity might be. Lord Campbell said that he meant it to be what it had always been and that work that even pretended to be literature or art had little to fear. All of this was nullified, however, by Lord Chief Justice Cockburn, who, in the now famous case of *Regina* v. *Hicklin,* decided in 1868, laid down this entrancing measure of obscenity: "I think the test of obscenity is this, whether the tendency of the matter charged as obscene is to deprave and corrupt those whose minds are open to such immoral influences, and into whose hands a publication of this sort may fall."

Strictly applied, this rule would put an end to current literature, since a moron could pervert to some sexual fantasy to which his mind is open the listings in a seed catalogue.

This case is still the law of England, but it is not enforced. Please remember that Anglo-Saxon law is not considered as divinely inspired, in the sense that Cicero meant when he said that law is something drawn from the forehead of the gods, ordering what is right and prohibiting what is wrong.

Hence our law is used as an anvil on which to hammer out our social experiments. If the experiment proves good, the law operates in full vigor; if it doesn't, we forget the law, but we also forget to repeal it. If the authorities let it be known that all of the moral laws now on the books would be enforced to the letter, public alarm would reach panic proportions. The English, with their love of settled tradition, are content to keep Lord Cockburn's test of obscenity and use it when occasion requires, in the light of modern conditions and the temper of the times.

In America, libel, blasphemy, and obscenity have become part of the criminal law, but not, at least in Pennsylvania, until the Criminal Code of 1860. The Renaissance had a bawdy breadth both in Europe and in its American reflection. I need recall only that the father of the Post Office, Benjamin Franklin, wrote and presumably mailed his "Letter of Advice to Young Men on the Proper Choosing of a Mistress," that Thomas Jefferson worried about the students at his new University of Virginia having a respectable brothel, and that Alexander Hamilton's adultery while holding public office created no great scandal. What fired the whole question of public decency in this country was the appearance of a gentleman named Anthony Comstock in about 1870 and the various Purity Leagues and Societies for the Suppression of Vice that followed him. The resulting hullaballoo over artistic propriety represents the hammering on the anvil, and it lasted from 1870 to 1933, when Judge Woolsey, in New York, quieted the matter by approving James Joyce's *Ulysses*. Since then the raids of the vice squad have become negligible, except possibly in Boston, although even there the question is becoming residual. The focus of censorship is swinging now to social ideologies. The Catholic

Church, however, still exercises an active censorship, within its own ranks, of plays, movies, and books which it deems sacrilegious or indecent, and it is very effective, particularly in the case of movies.

It is interesting that no obscenity case involving current and widely marketed literature reached the Pennsylvania courts until 1949, when nine novels were the cause of a group of booksellers being arrested. These books were declared not obscene by the Court, although they contain the full panoply of passion, including descriptions of rape and lust and all of the four-letter pornography ever invented by the English tongue. This statement bears a bit of explanation.

*   *   *

Of all forms of expression, words are the most cherished and the most suspect. There is a constant strain between the right of free speech and the fear of it. This is because half the time we don't know what we're talking about—partly because we simply don't know and partly because our language is an imperfect vehicle, like a carriage with oval wheels. Painting and sculpture stay in one place, and certainly marble and bronze are a cold medium for communicating violent passion. You may read suggestions into both forms, but they are static. Words can do things in the dark that these other art forms cannot approach. And when we speak, our worst fear is the implied compulsion not only to speak freely but to speak fully—which is a frightening thing. Nothing less than the whole truth will do, in the long run, and hence our trouble is more with free truth than free speech.

The odd thing about truth is that it keeps changing its clothes. If you must insist on knowing what truth is, Holmes said that it was what he couldn't help thinking, with the added surmise that his "can't helps" weren't necessarily cosmic. In the field of censorship, it is largely a matter of what is agitating society at the moment: freedom of expression is always dimmest in the area of the fighting faiths. Let us not forget that *Don Quixote* was once burned because of the sentence: "Works of Charity negligently performed are of no worth"; that within our lifetime an editor deleted the word "chaste" because it was suggestive; that *Tom Sawyer* and *Huckleberry Finn* were once charged with corrupting the morals of children; that *Jane Eyre* was called too immoral to be ranked with decent literature, the *Scarlet Letter* a brokerage of lust, *Adam Bede* the vile outpourings of a lewd woman's mind; and that Walt Whitman lost his government job because of his *Leaves of Grass*. We laugh at these things now, just as we laughed a generation ago at calling a man a Communist—but just try doing that today.

Thus truth shifts, or its forms do. If obscenity had a fixed meaning, it should apply uniformly and have a discernible and constant effect. Yet our museums are filled with statues and pictures of people as naked as a billiard ball. Comstock once had his fling at art and had the reputable Knoedler Galleries raided in 1887: and, static though it be, if you don't think that painting or drawing is susceptible of eroticism, look at the work of George Grosz. Pope Pius IV was once shocked by Michelangelo's fresco of The Last Judgment in the Sistine Chapel and ordered loin-cloths put on the figures. Where is such horror now? Thousands of people go to the museums of this country every day, and no one turns into a satyr.

* * *

Music, oddly enough, has escaped almost scot-free. I doubt that it could have been a problem before modern times, for who could arouse much passion with a rebec, a bombard, or a three-stringed lute? Even so, the Church was suspicious of it and did not capitulate to the pipe-organ until fairly late in its history, less on moral grounds than because music distracts from the direct contemplation of brimstone. My feeling is that music is by far the least understood of the arts and the one with most inherent distractions. In itself it is wholly evanescent: it is heard and is gone, but this probably intensifies its power of fantasy. To hear it, however, one must be in public, watching a group of sober people, slightly perspiring and bug-eyed, straining at their instruments, or one is part of an uncomfortable crowd of wriggling humanity on a dance floor. These things take off the erotic edge. I shall speak in a minute of radio and record music that can, like a book, be listened to in seclusion.

I doubt that people ever know when music is erotic, and this is indeed a mystery, since music is based on rhythm, that most primitive of compulsions. Take Wagner's *Venusberg* music, which is sex set straight to music, or its idealization in the second movement of Beethoven's *Seventh Symphony*. And much jazz is as frankly erotic as the Bridal and Circumcision Rites of the Watusi—perhaps more so, since the savages make a ceremonial of natural phenomena. Nevertheless, even if people do not recognize what is happening to them, it happens just the same, and I think that jazz has a great deal to do with unconsidered romance and marriage. It certainly furthers the idea that if two young people get together they will automatically be true to each other, at least for a little while. Perhaps bebop is a healthy rebellion against all this, or is it only the substitution of one form of lunacy for another? I suggest it in full awareness of what George Moore said—that if the censors should succeed in sweeping from the face of the earth every vestige of material that might conceivably tend to arouse the emotions of sex, the spring breeze would remain to quicken the pulses of men and women.

Music, then, escapes the censor becauses it isn't understood. Dr. Johnson called it "the only sensual pleasure without vice." I recall when Shostakovitch's *Lady Macbeth of Mtsensk* was given in Philadelphia. The performance was not allowed to go on unless a curtain was put up around a certain bedroom scene, but the music, which was extraordinarily suggestive, was left untouched. No point could be made from this, however, because in the middle of the scene, with only the music going unabated, the curtain fell down, to reveal the two actors who had disappeared behind it taking advantage of the unexpected breather by removing only their wigs.

❉   ❉   ❉

But the word, spoken and written, remains the villain in the piece of modern censorship, together with the scenes that words suggest on the screen and in the theatre. At this point a most important factor must be observed. Private censorship takes over from the law in direct proportion to the circulation of the material. The more people a medium of expression reaches, the purer it gets by voluntary action. This brings in the secluded listening to radio and records that I mentioned a moment ago. For all of Milton and his *Areopagitica,* and despite the constant furore over free speech, pre-publication licensing still exists throughout the nation in the case of motion pictures.

Since 1915, when the movies became a medium of general public entertainment, it has been the law in Pennsylvania and elsewhere that no motion picture can be shown until it has been approved by the State Board of Censors. This legislation has been upheld by the United States Supreme Court. Why don't we get furious at this violation of our Anglo-Saxon liberties? The answer is that the motion picture industry censors itself far more severely than the State Board would think of doing or dare to do. A kiss may not last for more than four feet of film, and language, clothing, and situations are minutely and rigidly limited by the producers' own code. The same is largely true of radio and wax recordings. The censor's approval is therefore only the faint echo of a rubber stamp.

Among the magazines, there is one with a weekly circulation of 4,000,000 which only within the past five years or so has agreed to take cigarette advertising and still refuses liquor displays. It also censors its own columns for language and situations that might offend the public's sense of decency. The big publishers know all about the public's sense of decency and do not need censors to tell them what it is. It is a matter of dollars and cents to them, for America is a very moral and religious nation. Don't be misled by the figures on divorce or illegitimate babies. The babies can be counted in terms of thousands: the reading, listening, and watching public in terms of dozens of millions. As for divorce, which now occurs in about one out of every four marriages, the cause of it is not sexual immorality as such. The cause of divorce is marriage, and divorce will not decrease until we have learned better how to marry.

There is an obvious difference between the purity of magazines, radio, and movies, on the one hand, and books and plays, on the other. I have said that the nine novels that were cleared of obscenity by the Philadelphia courts had in them all the bad words and horrid situations. Two things make this possible. In the first place, it is the rare book that has a circulation of a million; the average is probably near ten thousand. There have been exceptions like *Forever Amber,* but Papini's *Life of Christ* was such an exception too. In the second place, American law says specifically that vulgarity is not enough and will not now allow the suppression of a book unless its purpose and effect, however vulgar, are also aimed at arousing and exciting sexual desires. This is the last thing that these mournful volumes do. They rather arouse feelings of horror or pity for the degradation of mankind, and few people would want to emulate the desolate characters that move through the pages of such books. The authors do attempt faithfully to portray what goes on in the shadowy places of our civilization. Who should say that an author must choose one locale rather than another, or that he should write only about nice people? The same is true of the theatre, which is now limited to the very largest metropolitan centers. While I have not seen the movie version of *Streetcar Named Desire,* I am willing to lay a small wager that it has been bowdlerized.

Books and plays, then, can safely be franker and more controversial than magazines and movies because of their narrower circulation. For the most part, people read books or they read magazines—the great mass of the public does not, generally speaking, read both. And few people ever read plays. This same consideration answers the apparent anomaly of books known as the classics. Comstock went after them, but long before the day of the vice-hunter was over the classics won protection from the law. Once a book is old enough to have acquired a firm grip on immortality, it loses its interest and is no longer read; it stands on our shelves like an old gun in a fort, much admired but not looked into. Yet an appalling amount of so-called immorality can be found in Shakespeare, Chaucer, Aristophanes, Juvenal, Ovid, Swift, Defoe, Fielding, Smollett, Rousseau, Maupassant, Voltaire, Balzac, Baudelaire, Rabelais, Swinburne, Shelley, Byron, Boccaccio, Hardy, Shaw, Whitman, and a host more. Annie Besant, when on trial for criminal obscenity in England, compiled a list of one hundred and fifty passages from the Bible that might fairly be considered obscene by the current standards of the times. It is enough to cite the story of Lot and his daughters, in Genesis.

It may be asked whether one would care to have one's daughter read books that contain frank eroticism. Let parents look to themselves for the answer to that. If they live normal lives so that their daughters' time is filled with the average amount of schooling, homework, and diversion, they will find that the young show no curiosity about the titles that look out unconcealed from the library shelves, from *Lady Chatterly's Lover* to Ellis's *Studies in the Psychology of Sex*. By the time they are old enough to want to read in this corner of the bookroom they will have learned the biologic facts of life and the words that go with them. There is something seriously wrong at home if these facts have not been met and sorted by then. I should prefer my own daughters to meet the life and literature of the world in my library than behind the neighbor's barn, for we cannot hold back the outcome of growth, and since life is a series of minor battles over major issues, the burden of choice is on each one of us, every day. Our daughters must live in the world and decide what sort of women they are to be, and I prefer their deliberate and informed choice of decency. If that choice be made in the open sunlight, it is more apt than when made in shadow to fall on the side of honorable behavior.

Plays have suffered at the hands of the censor as much as books, and perhaps more so. Long after pre-publication licensing of books was abandoned, the pre-production censorship of plays persisted. Such a system existed in France until 1906 and even later in some other European countries. In England the Lord Chamberlain performed this function at least until the last war. In New York there was a Play Jury, but in 1927 the Legislature passed the Wales Act, since repealed, which provided for padlocking for an entire year any theatre that was rented for the production of a play that might later be declared obscene. The officials of most communities can stop a play, under their general police power, if they have reason or even a reasonable fear to believe that it will result in a breach of the peace. I myself upheld the Mayor's ban on *Mulatto* about ten years ago, when the police were able to produce such evidence. Being presented before a crowd, a play is capable of raising a riot more easily than a book.

*   *   *

Really to come to grips with the question of obscenity is like coming to grips with a greased pig. How it affects people, and when, where, why, and whether it does at all are hard questions to answer: so too are what actually is the effect, who is to say, and whose standards are to be applied. When a man's sensuality is high, a nursery rhyme may excite him: when it is low, the most obscene material may bore him. Should one book be censored and the other not, in that ex-

ample, and if so, which? The best that the lawmakers can do
is to rest the whole business generally on common sense, and
to conclude, regretfully or otherwise, that obscenity has a
mystic and self-executing power to harm. That is about
where the matter rests now, without anyone paying much
attention to it. We are not apt to be thrown off balance by
Esquire when we are worrying about the hydrogen bomb.

But I must enter a caveat. The law against obscenity may
slumber, but we will always have one to deal with. There is
a First Amendment to the Federal Constitution, which guar-
antees the freedom of speech, but there is also a Fifth, which
proscribes the taking of life, liberty, or property without due
process of law: this lets in the police power. Some people are
afraid that the Fifth Amendment may swallow up the First,
since a great deal of police power is constitutionally possible,
provided it observe due process. Alexander Meiklejohn, in
his book *Free Speech and Its Relation to Self-Government*,
draws a thoughtful distinction between public and private
speech, and advocates absolute exemption for all public expression without exception. As for private speech, suppression is logical enough if a breach of the peace results, hard
as that may be to prove. It becomes an interesting question
whether any book that makes substantial pretense to being
of general interest, even if published commercially, is not a
form of public expression and hence entitled to complete
exemption on that account alone.

Since we cannot expect to get along without a censorship
law, I advocate one that should prosecute only the possession,
publication, and sale of material depicting sexual acts, except-
ing medical and educational texts. This would take care of
dirty pictures and their literary equivalents. The Courts
would undoubtedly expand the field of such a law by inter-

preting the phrase "sexual acts" to include depicted situations so suggestive as to be tantamount to a sexual act. But in this day and age judges would not stray far in that direction, and at least the law would have a clear and honest start. Any other sort of law, involving such words as obscenity, morals of youth, moral turpitude, or common decency, should provide that the publication be tried first, as is now done in Massachusetts, and not the dealer or publisher, as is done in Pennsylvania; but such a law leaves on our hands the semantic wilderness of the meaning of obscenity, morals, decency, and turpitude.

We think we know instinctively what these words mean, but do we? If you will try to write out a definition of them, I suggest that you cannot do so without ultimately resting your definition upon the inherent decency and common sense of mankind. This leaves the matter precisely where it was at first, because throughout history the forms and conceptions of decency have changed and mankind's common sense has shifted, under pressure, from one area of behavior to another. I venture to assert that there are only two constant attributes of human life—love and a conviction of the Divine. Since we are born whole, we must live whole, and I do not believe that salvation rests in any one section of the mind, the spirit, or the body, but that it comes with entire and integrated living.

It seems to me that the whole question of legal censorship comes down to whether we have faith in people or whether we fear they won't have the courage and moral stamina of our convictions. The State of New Mexico has no law against obscenity, but the New Mexicans don't seem to rush periodically into the streets and engage in orgiastic riots. If we make an article contraband by law, we do not stop the traffic in it; we merely force the price up and make it a more lucrative business. The body politic, like the human body, will always have its ulcers, which tend to seal themselves off. They need be lanced only when they threaten the peace and good order of the body generally. What danger can befall us so long as the public has the chance to answer back? Justice Brandeis said in the case of *Whitney* v. *California:* "No danger flowing from speech can be deemed clear and present, unless the incidence of the evil apprehended is so imminent that it may befall before there is opportunity for full discussion." As we have seen, the public answers its own big questions, like the decency of the radio, the screen, and the magazines.

* * *

I have said that the focus of restriction is turning lately to social ideologies. For the first time we are being forced to take seriously the power and breadth of the growing rebellion against our individual liberties and our system of property. Public servants and educators are being required to take an oath of loyalty. This is no new device, since people swore fealty to their feudal lords throughout the Middle Ages under the same general compulsions and for the same general reasons. But to the modern mind it is alarming to find that the censoring law has taken a positive rather than a negative form. Yet we are not alarmed by laws that require food that is sold commercially to be of a certain purity. What is the difference between a pure food law and á pure faith law? Surely we know that the Constitution to which we now must swear allegiance was created as part of a revolt against royal tyranny and not against our system of private property and privileges, and that its protection is the same, with or without an oath. Is our alarm based on a desire to turn anarchist at any time we want to? Surely we would take the oath and the loss of our jobs as minor annoyances, if that were our decision. Do we dislike the oath because we are afraid of our own officials? But thus far America, with ballot box and public wrath, has been able to take petty tyrants in her stride and dispose of them, knowing that she has slowly been righting her own wrongs. Why are we more afraid of Senator McCarthy than we were of Huey Long?

I think the answer lies in our fear of a new kind of mastery whose challenge, according to the point of view, is either that we define our faith and live up to it or else that we hand over its fruits to someone who wants them and may be strong enough to take them.

What would happen if we began to live up to the letter of our chartered liberty—both its rights and its disciplines? Are we not more than a little fearful that the power of our heart is not yet equal to the power of our inventive mind? The challenge is coming to us from abroad, from strange people whose ways we do not understand; it is coming like a gale of wind, and it is hard to put handcuffs on a gale of wind. Remember the Lord Chancellor in *Iolanthe,* suggesting an affidavit from a thunderstorm or some evidence from a heavy shower. When we lift the lid from our own soul, are we not secretly alarmed at some of the winds that blow out of it? What is happening today is that we are being forced to look there.

Deserving liberty is a very difficult business, merely having it is easy and comfortable. One of its main tenets is that we live without fear; when we can do that we will have begun to be free men.

I do not like the loyalty oath, but its importance fades in the growing glare of the general challenge. We do not like to have our loyalty questioned; we do not like the threat of domination of our minds. We have beaten Hitler, or have we? Have we also beaten Genghis Khan? We must remember that the growing swarms of people in the world must ride across the boundaries of their famine in one way or another. What is in our minds: what *is* our loyalty? How have we used our trust? These questions will grow more urgent, not less; how long do we think we can afford to answer them to ourselves alone? They will continue to be asked, whether by loyalty oaths or otherwise, because it is the condition of the world that asks them. It is not the oath that we dislike, for we must expect to be challenged; but we properly mistrust the abuse of power by those who can use the oath as litmus paper to judge the coloration of what we say or do next. This we can protest against, object to, and raise a row about; and we must do what we can to supplant the ruffians who misuse a power so delicate. They are not merely the sort of gangsters we are used to. They are still our own people but with a chill on them—the ominous chill of a universal tyranny that is the more fearful because it is partly native and partly from the outer void. In short, the potential despot that is in every man threatens to become a real figure in local and international politics. The gale is seeking out the crevices of all our houses. This is a bit outside the field of my assignment, and I have no pat answer: but we can keep a stout heart and do battle, beginning with ourselves.

❋ ❋ ❋

I pause now to draw a long breath and to conclude briefly. We are quite used to the idea of censorship, for we are subjected to it every day of our lives. The civil and criminal codes, the tax law, Emily Post, custom, and habit are all

forms of censorship. Every time we are held up by a red traffic light our freedom of action is censored. At the bottom of
the law's imposing list of *Don'ts* stand our few pale and timid
moral laws. These are the merest foothills to the world of the
spirit: the upper ranges are the great poetry, music, philosophy, stories, and inventions that have come from the mind
of man. If we must—as of course we must—keep our machin-
ery turning and our gutters clean, we must also lift up our
eyes unto the hills. My speech has spun principally around
the obscene or vulgar word, which is the raw spot to which
censorship has been applied in our era. But when we think
of the world's great literature we are in clearer and more
lovely air. It can do all that obscenity can to forward an
understanding of life, and do it better. I cannot make as good
a plea for it as another has done. In 1903 there appeared an
anonymous book called *Letters from a Chinese Official,* pur-
portedly written by a Chinese and sharply criticizing the
West. Years later, an Englishman confessed to it, and I
know no lovelier writing. I shall close by letting him tell
you about literature and living:

Our poets and literary men have taught their successors, for long
generations, to look for good not in wealth, not in power, not
in miscellaneous activity, but in a trained, a choice, an exquisite
appreciation of the most simple and universal relations of life. To
feel, and in order to feel to express, or at least to understand the
expression of all that is lovely in Nature, of all that is poignant
and sensitive in man, is to us in itself a sufficient end. A rose in a
moonlit garden, the shadow of trees on the turf, almond bloom,
scent of pine, the wine-cup and the guitar; these and the pathos
of life and death, the long embrace, the hand stretched out in
vain, the moment that glides forever away, with its freight of
music and light, into the shadow and hush of the haunted past,
all that we have, all that eludes us, a bird on the wing, a perfume

escaped on the gale—to all these things we are trained to respond and the response is what we call literature. This we have; this you cannot give us; but this you may so easily take away. Amid the roar of looms it cannot be heard; it cannot be seen in the smoke of factories; it is killed by the wear and the whirl of Western life. And when I look at your business men, the men whom you most admire; when I see them hour after hour, day after day, year after year, toiling in the mill of their forced and undelighted labors; when I see them importing the anxieties of the day into their scant and grudging leisure, and wearing themselves out less by toil than by carking and illiberal cares, I reflect, I confess, with satisfaction on the simpler routine of our ancient industry, and prize, above all your new and dangerous routes, the beaten track so familiar to our accustomed feet that we have leisure, even while we pace it, to turn our gaze up to the eternal stars.

James P. Baxter, III

FREEDOM IN EDUCATION

W HY should the last of the freedoms to be discussed in this series of Cooper lectures be "Freedom in Education"? Certainly not because it is of the least importance, for it underlies all the others, and anything that weakens it necessarily threatens them. It affects teachers and students more directly than the other freedoms, but it affects everyone who has a stake in the advancement and dissemination of knowledge. The recent attack on freedom at the University of California concerns not only the citizens of that great state but you and me. It was a former regent of that University, the late Chester A. Rowell, who described freedom in education as " the central liberty of civilization without which no other liberty could long survive or would be worth keeping."[1]

Freedom in education is supremely important because of its genetic relationship to the other freedoms. If the free spirit of inquiry did not prevail in our colleges and universities, where would we find our champions of freedom of speech like Professor Chafee, or our champions of freedom in literature like Judge Bok? Totalitarian rulers have paid a high

[1] George R. Stewart, *The Year of the Oath* (Garden City, New York, 1950), p. 19.

tribute to the educational world by moving rapidly, as soon as they grasp the helm of the state, to get their hands on the universities, and thereby dam up the spirit of liberty at its fountainhead. Any manual for dictators would lay stress on seizing the educational system as promptly as the central power stations and the arsenals. All three of these targets are essential in both the defense and the overthrow of freedom. In the defense of liberty our colleges and universities have proved themselves to be both arsenals and power stations. As soon as Mussolini, Hitler, and Stalin got effective control of the universities they found it easier to overthrow liberty in other areas of their nations.

The tradition of academic freedom is an ancient one. The teachers of America, like the teachers of France or Great Britain, are the spiritual descendants of the companies of scholars who in the late Middle Ages constituted the great universities which became the dynamos of our Western culture. These scholars were free to seek truth and to teach and publish it, because without freedom their function would be meaningless. There is an analogy here between the status of a scholar and the status of an ambassador. In the slow and halting development of international law, one of the first principles to win general acceptance was the idea that the person of the ambassador must be safe from violence. Otherwise he would be not the representative of his sovereign but the dependent of the court to which he was accredited, and diplomatic negotiations would become at once impossible. In much the same way, men came to see that if the scholar were to perform his function of seeking and imparting truth, he had to be free to speak his mind, and to affirm that the world, after all, did move. Our colleges and universities, like those of Europe, are still companies of scholars whose activities become as meaningless as those of an unsafe ambassador unless they are free to seek truth and impart it.

These companies of scholars long ago developed a code of ethics as important and as effective as that of the medical profession. A professor who sold an examination paper, forged a document, or corrupted the morals of a student would be at once dismissed by the administrative authorities. The loss of his job and the difficulty of finding another would weigh no more heavily on him than the contempt of his fellow scholars, who would turn on him with the sentiments a marine would feel for a comrade that ran from battle.

"Truth is great," declared Thomas Jefferson, "and will prevail if left to herself. She is the proper and sufficient antagonist of error and has nothing to fear from the conflict unless, by human interposition, disarmed of her natural weapons— free argument and debate; errors ceasing to be dangerous when it is permitted freely to contradict them."[2] As the coping stone to his life work, Jefferson founded the University of Virginia, dedicated to the advancement of truth by the free use of the human reason, as distinguished from conclusions based on custom or revelation or authority. Interestingly enough, the first appointment to the Virginia faculty provoked an outburst of criticism in the State legislature, for the eminent scholar Dr. Thomas Cooper had been prosecuted under the Sedition Law, and had also been denounced as a Unitarian.

Under pressure from certain religious leaders, Dr. Cooper lost his job; but as time went on the battle for Jefferson's ideas of freedom in education continued to gain ground. As far as I can discover no teacher at Williams College has ever

2 Howard M. Jones, *Primer of Intellectual Freedom* (Cambridge, Mass., 1949), p. 145.

been dismissed for his opinions since the college opened its doors in 1793. A Williams song describes the college as "renowned for baseball and free trade," the latter an allusion to Professor Arthur Latham Perry, the father of Bliss and of Lewis. This colorful economist, enshrined in Williams tradition as "Historical Peri," was attacked by a group of alumni in 1883 for opposing the protective tariff, but the Board of Trustees gave the petition the treatment it deserved.[3]

During the First World War and directly following it, there developed an hysterical attack on teachers and on history textbooks that reminds one of the jitters from which many Americans have been suffering since 1939. Our entry into war with Germany made us acutely aware of the dangers of hyphenism and suspicious of the loyalty of our German-American citizens, as we were later to be suspicious of our Japanese-American citizens. It is interesting to note that the 32d Division, composed of troops from the Old Northwest, many of whom came from German-speaking families, proved itself one of the finest of American divisions, with a deserved reputation for gallantry under fire which was emulated by so many of the Nisei in World War II. In both periods, however, the American people were fearful, intolerant, and too often guilty of conduct that now seems shameful and ridiculous in the strongest and most secure of the great democracies. A visiting British journalist described the American public mind of 1919 as "hagridden by the specter of Bolshevism. . . . Property was in an agony of fear, and the horrid name 'Radical' covered the most innocent departure from conventional thought with a suspicion of desperate purpose.

[3] Arthur L. Perry, *Williamstown and Williams College*, c. 1899, pp. 697-708.

'America,' as a wit of the time said, 'is the land of liberty—liberty to keep in step.' "[4]

Suspicion turned against teachers just as it turned against Americans of foreign extraction. Bessie Pierce, whose study entitled *Public Opinion and the Teaching and History* has become an American classic, found that the superintendents of public instruction in thirty-two states reported that no accusations involving the loyalty of teachers were brought to their attention from 1917 to 1924. Under the Lusk Law in New York, however, several public schoolteachers were dismissed when they failed to obtain a certificate of loyalty. One of these, Miss Mary McDowell, a Quakeress, despite thirteen years of excellent service in the Brooklyn schools, was dismissed in June 1918 simply because of her pacifist views. Five years later she was reinstated.[5]

* * *

In 1921-22, having recently recovered from a long illness, I taught history part-time in a well-known small college in Colorado. My wife came back from a luncheon one day and told me that her hostess had delivered a tirade against teachers in general. "But shouldn't teachers be allowed to say what they think?" Mrs. Baxter inquired. "Of course they should, my dear," replied her hostess, "they should be encouraged to do so. Then if they're not thinking properly, they can be discharged."

As a Republican from Maine I happened to be above suspicion, but I had a first-hand opportunity to see what damage a denial of freedom can do to an outstanding small

[4] A. G. Gardiner, *Portraits and Portents* (New York, 1926), p. 13.
[5] Pierce, *op. cit.* (New York, 1926), pp. 111-31.

college. The trustees had not long before dismissed without a hearing the dean of the college, who had served with distinction as chairman of the English department for the past twenty-five years. In the resulting controversy one trustee remarked that no professor, regardless of seniority, had any more right to his job than a manual laborer in a copper mine. The dismissed dean soon became the president of an Ohio college. Two distinguished professors promptly resigned to take over the chairmanships of the Departments of Romance Languages and of Mathematics at the University of California. Two others moved to Wesleyan, and another joined the staff of the Harvard Business School. These resignations were serious blows to the college, but not so serious, perhaps, as the decline in morale of the teachers who remained.

I left Colorado in 1922 for graduate study at Harvard. As a teacher there from 1925 to 1937, I had an opportunity to see just how strong a contribution could be made to faculty zest for teaching and research by a championship of freedom in education. President Lowell's statement of the case in his annual report for 1916-17 had become a classic.

Experience has proved, and probably no one would now deny, that knowledge can advance, or at least can advance most rapidly, only by means of an unfettered search for truth on the part of those who devote their lives to seeking it in their respective fields, and by complete freedom in imparting to their pupils the truth that they have found. This has become an axiom in higher education, in spite of the fact that a searcher may discover error instead of truth, and be misled and mislead others thereby. We believe that if light enough is let in, the real relations of things will soon be seen, and that they can be seen in no other way.[6]

[6] Henry A. Yeomans, *Abbott Lawrence Lowell* (Cambridge, Mass., 1948), p. 308.

Mr. Lowell pointed out that beyond his chosen field and outside his classroom a professor speaks only as a citizen and should be free to express his opinions even though his injudicious remarks may sometimes injure the institution with which he is connected. Mr. Lowell asserted that

In spite, however, of the risk of injury to the institution, the objections to restraint upon what professors may say as citizens seem to me far greater than the harm done by leaving them free. In the first place, to impose upon the teacher in a university restrictions to which the members of other professions, lawyers, physicians, engineers, and so forth, are not subjected, would produce a sense of irritation and humiliation. In accepting a chair under such conditions a man would surrender a part of his liberty; what he might say would be submitted to the censorship of a board of trustees, and he would cease to be a free citizen. . . . That is an objection to restraint on freedom of speech from the standpoint of the teacher. There is another, not less weighty, from that of the institution itself. If a university or college censors what its professors may say, if it restrains them from uttering something that it does not approve, it thereby assumes responsibility for that which it permits them to say. This is logical and inevitable, but it is a responsibility which an institution of learning would be very unwise in assuming. It is sometimes suggested that the principles are different in time of war; that the governing boards are then justified in restraining unpatriotic expressions injurious to the country. But the same problem is presented in war time as in time of peace. If the university is right in restraining its professors, it has a duty to do so, and it is responsible for whatever it permits. There is no middle ground.

Having seen with my own eyes the damage done to a fine Colorado college by an attack on academic freedom, I could better appreciate how much the championship of freedom by Presidents Lowell and Conant did to strengthen the Harvard faculties, help to attract outstanding scholars, and hold them against competing offers. When I became a college president myself in 1937 these lessons were fresh in my mind. In my induction address I pointed out that freedom in education had been destroyed in Russia, Italy and Germany and had been attacked too often in our own country. The true course seemed to me that indicated by Justice Holmes' dissenting opinion in the Abrams case.

When men have realized that time has upset many fighting faiths, they may come to believe . . . that the ultimate good desired is better reached by free trade in ideas—that the best test of truth is the power of the thought to get itself accepted in the competition of the market, and that truth is the only ground upon which their wishes safely can be carried out. That, at any rate, is the theory of our Constitution.

Holmes put this point still more sharply in *U. S.* vs. *Schwimmer,* declaring that "if there is any principle of the Constitution that more imperatively calls for attachment than any other, it is the principle of free thought—not free thought for those who agree with us but freedom for the thought that we hate."

Ever since I was asked to give this lecture I have been pondering these classic formulations by Justice Holmes of the age-old problem of freedom vs. authority. I have asked myself whether thirteen years of experience in administering the affairs of a college has changed my viewpoint. I think it has. I am more deeply convinced than ever of the soundness of Holmes' views, but experience has shown me that a large portion of our countrymen reject them. It is significant that Holmes' opinions in both the Abrams and the Schwimmer case were dissents.

*   *   *

Why is it that so many Americans do not share the views of Milton, Jefferson, and Holmes that truth is mighty and will prevail? There have always been large numbers of men who prefer "thought control" to freedom, men who are eager —as Walter Bagehot has pointed out—to use the "immense engine" of the State "to crush the errors which they hate, and to replace them with the tenets they approve."[7] President Conant gave an explanation of their reasons in his book, *Education in a Divided World,* published in 1948.

Those who worry about radicalism in our schools and colleges are often either reactionaries who themselves do not bear allegiance to the traditional American principles, or defeatists who despair of the success of our own philosophy in an open competition. The first group are consciously or unconsciously aiming at a transformation of this society, perhaps initially not as revolutionary or violent as that which the Soviet agents envisage, but one eventually equally divergent from our historic goals. The others are unduly timid about the outcome of a battle of *ideas;* they lack confidence in our own intellectual armament. . . . They often fail to recognize that diversity of opinion within the framework of loyalty to our free society is not only basic to a university but to the entire nation. For in a democracy with our traditions only those reasoned convictions which emerge from diversity of opinion can lead to that unity and national solidity so essential for the welfare of our country—essential not only for our own security but even more a requisite for intelligent action toward the end we all desire, namely, the conversion of the present armed truce into a firm and lasting peace.

In my opinion, recent history has colored our thinking about thought control. Because we saw despotism triumph in Italy, Germany, and Russia, many of us came to fear the power of the big lie more than the power of the big battalions. The advances that have been made in the art of lying during my lifetime seem to me to be as dangerous

7 "The Metaphysical Basis of Toleration," cited in Jones, *Primer of Intellectual Freedom,* p. 80.

potentially as the advances in nuclear physics. Propaganda had a long background before you and I learned to read and to listen, but recent developments in two widely different research fields, psychology and electrical communications, stepped up its power. Analyzing man's fears and frustrations, the psychologist showed how rumors, innuendoes, half truths and the grossest falsehoods could be used to stampede men like cattle headed for a precipice. The psychologist furnished Goebbels with devilish insights. At the same time the physicist and the communications engineer magnified his power a thousandfold.

We made no mistake in fearing the skill of the Nazis and of the Communists in psychological warfare. While I served as deputy director of the Office of Strategic Services in 1941 and 1942, I saw many of the intercepted instructions which were sent from the director of the German apparatus within this country to his agents here, and I marveled at the skill with which the flaws in our democratic life—anti-Semitism, anti-Catholicism, anti-Negroism—were turned to enemy advantage.

Where we have erred, it seems to me, is in underestimating and misjudging the means at our disposal to combat communism. At a hearing at the State House in Boston some years ago, a proponent of a teachers' oath bill asked me if I didn't agree with him that a single Communist or fellow traveler could destroy a faculty as surely as a rotten apple in a barrel. I retorted that a quarter century spent in teaching had convinced me that professors are as little like apples in a barrel as anything one could imagine. Where ideas were concerned, it would be hard to find anything less passive than a college faculty. Controversy is the breath of their nostrils. Half or more of any typical college faculty would have worn their country's uniform in World War I or World War II. Though some of them might now be too old for foxholes, they never were—and never will be—too old to wield a vigorous shillelagh in the battle of ideas.

Indeed it is easier to mobilize our intellectuals for that sort of contest than to mobilize anyone else. Their attitude reminds me of that of native Coloradoans toward the rattlesnake. Having grown up in Maine, which is as free from venomous serpents as Ireland itself, I regarded rattlesnakes, when I moved to Colorado in quest of health, as something one might well pass by on the other side. Then I married a Colorado girl and learned to my surprise that anyone who met a rattler was supposed to kill it. "It might otherwise hurt a child," my wife explained. Since scholars have just the same feeling about falsehoods, it did not take me long to get the point.

The idea of protecting society against dangerous thoughts by the imposition of teachers' oaths is an unfortunate outcome of the jittery state of public opinion in the past two decades. The oath required of teachers in public and private institutions in Massachusetts runs as follows: "I do solemnly swear (or affirm) that I will support the Constitution of the United States and the Constitution of the Commonwealth of Massachusetts, and that I will faithfully discharge the duties of the position of . . . . in . . . . according to the best of my ability." Educators objected to it because they saw no reason why it should be exacted of them as a class, but it has done little harm, and presumably very little good, in the years I've watched it operate. Against Communists, it is less effective than a toy pistol. Indeed a Communist Party member might get the same zest from false swearing that a Boy Scout gets from his good deed of the day. In such a group of idealistic individualists as a college faculty, however, there is always the risk that someone completely free from any suspicion of radicalism may have conscientious scruples about a required oath, and thereby be lost to the teaching profession.

*   *   *

A tragic illustration of this principle is afforded by the University of California, one of the greatest of our universities.[8] Because of the eminence of its faculties, most scholars would have been inclined in 1950 to rank it in the top five American universities and some would have placed it in the top three. Very few made so great a contribution toward the winning of World War II.

Teachers at the University of California, like other public officials, take the oath provided in the state constitution in the following words: "I do solemnly swear (or affirm) that I will support the Constitution of the United States and the Constitution of the State of California, and that I will faithfully discharge the duties of my office according to the best of my ability." The State Constitution provides that "no other oath, declaration, or test, shall be required as a qualification for any office or public trust."

The Board of Regents adopted a resolution in October 1940 excluding members of the Communist Party from employment in the University but did not proceed against any individuals under that provision. On June 24, 1949, they decided to implement their anti-Communist policy by requiring of all employees a new oath, including the words, "I am not a member of the Communist Party, or under any

---

[8] Besides Stewart, *The Year of the Oath*, see the Petition for Writ of Mandate with supporting points and authorities, and the Petitioners' Reply Brief in *Tolman et al.* vs. *Underhill*, 3 Civil No. 7946, California, 1950.

oath, or a party to any agreement, or under any commitment that is in conflict with my obligations under this oath."

Some members of the University of California faculty were disposed to argue that since the Communist Party was a legal party in California, this oath constituted a political test for membership in the faculty, and was therefore contrary to the spirit, if not the letter, of the State Constitution, and that a blanket prohibition against all Communists constituted a recognition of "guilt by association." A large majority of the faculty, however, took the view that the commitments taken by all Communists deprive them of any right to a place in the company of scholars. This view was expressed in a resolution of March 7, 1950, which passed the Northern Section of the Academic Senate by a vote of 724 to 203, and the Southern Section by a vote of 301 to 65. It is important to recognize that the opponents of the new oath fully recognized that loyalty to any doctrine of totalitarianism shackles the free pursuit of truth. The March 7 resolution states this bluntly: "No person whose commitments or obligations to any organization, Communist or other, prejudice impartial scholarship and the free pursuit of truth will be employed by the University. Proved members of the Communist Party, by reason of such commitments to that party, are not acceptable as members of the faculty."[9] The faculty opponents of the new oath stressed the traditional right of teachers to be judged by their peers as to ability and integrity, and declared that once their privilege to teach became dependent on signing superimposed statements, their capacity to teach, freely and honestly, was imperiled.

The ensuing controversy attracted nation-wide attention. In April 1950, through the mediation of an alumni commit-

[9] Stewart, *The Year of the Oath*, pp. 37-38, 148.

tee, a compromise was reached, by which every employee of the University should take the constitutional oath and then sign a letter accepting his annual appointment in which he stated, as a consideration of payment of his salary: "I am not a member of the Communist Party or any other organization which advocates the overthrow of the Government by force or violence, and . . . I have no commitments in conflict with my responsibilities with respect to impartial scholarship and free pursuit of truth."

The compromise provided that non-signers might petition through the President for a hearing by the Committee on Privilege and Tenure of the Academic Senate, after which the Regents would consider the findings and recommendations of the Committee and the President before making a decision. Thirty-nine non-signers, who had been cleared by this Committee of any taint of communism, were appointed to their respective positions on July 21 by vote of a 10-to-9 majority of the Regents, including both President Sproul and Governor Warren. At a subsequent meeting on August 25, the Regents by a vote of 12 to 10, with President Sproul and Governor Warren this time in the minority, voted to rescind the appointments.[10] The legality of this action is now being tested in the courts, but the damage to the university has reached serious proportions. Professor John D. Hicks, a distinguished historian, summed up the case in a letter to one of the regents: "If any member of the thirty-nine non-signers were tainted with communism, I would be against him. But the integrity of these men . . . many of them scholars of world renown . . . has been abundantly proved." He bitterly predicted the consequence of the Regents' action: "There will be few resignations, for most of us cannot

[10] Petition for Writ of Mandate, in *Tolman et al.* vs. *Underhill.*

afford that luxury, but gradually the valuable men on our faculty will accept calls elsewhere, while our efforts to recruit competent scholars from the outside will fail (as they are already failing). The same dry-rot that has virtually destroyed the University of Texas, following a similar episode, will set in at California."[11]

According to a compilation, made recently by the faculty committee on academic freedom, the University of California has already lost one hundred ten scholars because of the loyalty oath controversy. This number includes twenty-six lost through dismissal, thirty-seven through resignation in protest against the action of the Regents, and forty-seven through refusal of offers of appointment to the California faculty.[12]

I have long maintained that there should be no place for Communists on a college or university faculty. My argument turns on the fact that the *minimum* requirements for Communist Party membership disqualify them from belonging to the company of scholars. They join a party of conspiratorial character which has at times advocated and perhaps still does advocate forcible overthrow of the government; which systematically practices falsehood and deceit; and which destroys free speech and other civil rights wherever it triumphs. All political parties contain liars, but it was left for the Communists and the Nazis to develop falsehood into a virtue and a chosen instrument of rule. It seems to me idle to argue that a man might be a Communist on part-time or on a basis of limited membership. What that Party demands of its members is, in Lenin's phrase, "the whole of their lives."

11 Pamphlet, *To Bring You the Facts,* August 1950, pp. 4-5.
12 *New York Times,* March 11, 1951.

The likelihood of a faculty member at Swarthmore or at Williams becoming a Communist is very slight indeed. Quite apart from other objectionable features of communism is the obvious fact of the suppression of freedom in education in Soviet Russia. But suppose for the sake of argument that a Williams teacher should avow himself a Communist? My duty, it seems to me, would be to recommend to our Board of Trustees that we suspend him from teaching and, if he were on a one- or three-year appointment, pay him to the end of his term. If he were on tenure without express limit of time, I would recommend that we suspend him from teaching, leaving him on pay during trial, proceed to establish the facts in a trial where he is represented by counsel, and, if the facts were established, terminate his contract, with such period of notice as seemed proper. He would presumably then sue us for breach of contract and it would be for the courts to say whether or not we had to pay him till age sixty-five, or whether we must pay him, in addition, damages for injury to his professional reputation. Different colleges seem to have had different legal opinions given them on this point. One of the ablest lawyers of the last generation, a life trustee of a great university, said that you could remove a professor for immorality but not for his opinions. If the courts held that view, I think it would be better to suspend an avowed Communist and pay him to age sixty-five than to have him teach.

* * *

The real difficulty that confronts American educators today has nothing to do with membership in the Communist Party but with the fact that non-Communist teachers at times say things that irritate prevailing sentiment and pro-

voke a barrage of abusive epithets. The history of attempts
to smear American liberals with the Red brush is long enough
to put us on our guard. When Mrs. Elizabeth Dilling published the first edition of her work, *The Red Network,*[13] a
newspaperman called on ex-Secretary of War Newton D.
Baker and asked him to comment on the inclusion of his
name in the list. Mr. Baker said that in his opinion "the
names of Jane Addams and Lillian D. Wald lent dignity to
the list."

The current fashion in smearing is to publish a list of
faculty members who have joined one or more organizations
listed by the Attorney General of the United States as "subversive" and to pad the list by including organizations to
which the faculty member under attack had never belonged,
and allegations long since refuted in hearings of legislative
bodies. The padding may comprise organizations with as
distinguished sponsorship as that of the Committee for a
Boycott against Japanese Aggression, which was headed by
that great American, Henry L. Stimson. I happened to
oppose the embargo, but can see no reason to conclude that
those who supported it were Reds.

Most Americans are unaware that when the Attorney
General lists an organization as "subversive" or as a "communist front," he makes clear that he is not affirming that
all its members are Communists, but simply that enough
Communists have bored from within to place that organization on his list. Like most of the rest of you, I have had the
experience of having one or more friends indicted by the
Federal authorities for conspiracy in restraint of trade, in
suits which the Government more often has lost than won.
I have always comforted myself with the thought that these

[13] April, 1934.

friends would have their day in court and would make good
use of it. Professor Chafee has pointed out that it is not so
easy for anyone who finds his name on the list of an organization branded by the Attorney General to get his day in
court. If an organization is ruled to be "subversive" by the
Department of Justice, gifts to it cease to be tax-exempt.
Conceivably there might be judicial review of the Department's ruling if a contributor to such an organization tried
to claim the contribution as a deduction on his income tax,
was refused, and got the issue before a court.

When a professor takes an unpopular stand someone is
likely to write to a college that they will not contribute to
its support unless the professor is dropped. One such letter
in 1949 provoked the memorable reply of Mr. Grenville
Clark of the Harvard Corporation: "I think it will always be
Harvard policy not to be influenced in any way 'to abridge
free speech' by the withholding of any subscription. . . . That
is what Mr. Eliot meant, I am sure, when he said, in 1869,
that while a university 'must be rich' it must 'above all' be
free."[14]

Within my thirteen years of experience people have made
similar threats concerning our Williams endowment campaigns, but we stuck by our guns and did whatever extra
work was necessary to put the campaigns over the top. I
recalled that individuals had likewise refused to support the
college as long as we had a Catholic or a Jew on the faculty,
as I am glad to say we have. Some have told me that the
real menace to education was not the Communist but the
Democratic Party. When one visiting journalist asked me
how many "New Dealers" we had on our Faculty, I replied,
Yankee fashion, "What is a New Dealer?" He defined it as

[14] *Harvard Alumni Bulletin,* June 25, 1949.

anyone who had worked for the Federal Government since 1933. I pointed out that this definition would include both me and my senior trustee. I added that although I, as a Maine Republican, could regard the appellation as simply amusing, my Senior Trustee, as a Pennsylvanian, would quite likely respond with a sock on the nose.

One thing that many of my correspondents fail to understand about freedom in education is revealed by the query as to why a professor who wishes to voice views that will embarrass the college in any way should not resign first, and then speak his piece. They say that it would be contrary to business ethics for the official of a company to take a public stand adverse to the interests of the company, and that if he felt he had to speak out to the company's hurt, he would first publicly sever his connection with it. My reply to this argument is that if I were in business I would certainly conform to that code and would expect my associates to do likewise. A college or university, on the other hand, can perform its essential functions only by assuring its faculty members of the right to speak their mind, without having either to resign beforehand, or to be dismissed afterward.

That does not mean, of course, that the professor has rights without responsibilities. The Association of American University Professors has pointed this out, in words that deserve repetition: "The college or university teacher is a citizen, a member of a learned profession, and an officer of an educational institution. Where he speaks or writes as a citizen, he should be free from institutional censorship or discipline, but his special position in the community imposes special obligations. As a man of learning and an educational officer, he should remember that the public may judge his profession and his institution by his utterances. Hence he should at all times be accurate, should exercise appropriate restraint, should show respect for the opinions of others, and should make every effort to indicate that he is not an institutional spokesman."[15]

                             *   *   *

Some of you may ask why it is I feel so strongly that there is no possible place for a Communist on a college or university faculty. Is it because I fear the ultimate success of communism in the fair competition of the market of ideas? Not in the least. I believe that we can beat them in arguments, and that we do wrong if we misdoubt the strength of truth. As my former student, Dean Wilbur J. Bender of Harvard, well put it:

We are not afraid of the enemies of democracy who are willing to express their ideas in the forum. We have confidence in the maturity and intelligence of [our] students. We have confidence in the strength of our free and dynamic American democracy. There is no danger from an open communist which is half as great as the danger from those who would destroy freedom in the name of freedom.[16]

In my opinion democracy in the State of Washington was not in peril whether three members of the Communist Party were to be retained on the Faculty, or dropped.

To my way of thinking, what was in peril in the Washington case was the fundamental assumption on which academic freedom rests: the assumption that the teacher is free to pursue truth, and has taken no commitments that disqualify him from membership in the company of scholars.

[15] American Association of University Professors, *Bulletin*, Spring, 1949, pp. 67-68.
[16] *Harvard Alumni Bulletin*, March 12, 1949.

Like President Raymond Allen, I happen to believe deeply in the responsibilities of the scholar, which are correlative to his rights to freedom. Those rights are guaranteed to him because only with freedom can truth be discovered and disseminated. The scholar must therefore be as free from the control of the Communist Party and its ideological line as he is free of pressure from any other source.

In Russia, scholars are not free to teach or to write the truth as they find it. They must conform strictly to the Marxist canon. Since World War II the Politburo has driven the intellectuals with a tight rein, condemning "bourgeois objectivity" and "art for art's sake" and insisting that all intellectual activities should be partisan. History, literature, philosophy, the social sciences and the fine arts, are all judged by their relation to the overriding concept of dialectical and historical materialism. A. A. Zhdanov, the spokesman for the Central Committee of the Communist Party, flung himself into this campaign with boundless zeal, denouncing "academic" and "objective" research as an unworthy occupation. Soviet scholars, he insisted, must be active Marxists, militant, partisan, and intolerant, free from "obsequiousness" and "subservience" to the bourgeois culture of the West.[17]

Most of the Soviet intellectuals came readily to heel. Their historians recognized that Marxist Leninism was the only admissible school of historical writing, and accepted Pokrovsky's dictum, "History is politics projected into the past." This means, of course, that history books must be tailored to fit the party line of the moment, and altered when the party line changes. For the writer's "evaluation of historical

[17] Sergius Yakobson, "Postwar Historical Research in the Soviet Union," *Annals of the American Academy of Political and Social Science* (Philadelphia, 1949), pp. 123-33.

facts is expected to be a political decision dictated by political considerations, and not the free objective judgment of an independent Western scholar." One well-known historian, Rubinstein, fawned on the regimenters, publishing an apology for having presented the historical theories of Lenin and Stalin as "the outcome of previously existing progressive historical thought instead of interpreting them as the foundation of an entirely new revolutionary science of history."[18] Small wonder that exaltation of Russia and defamation of foreigners and foreign countries have reached new highs. Alexander Fadeyev, secretary of the Union of Soviet Writers, attacking T. S. Eliot and other Western men of letters, remarked that "if hyenas could use fountain pens and jackals could use typewriters, this is how they would write."[19]

The Russian insistence on state control of musical compositions reminds me of the delightful bit of whimsy in the *Areopagitica* where Milton asks why the state should not censure music as well as letters. "It will ask more than the work of twenty licensers to examine all the lutes, the violins and the guitars in every house; they must not be suffered to prattle as they do, but must be licensed what they may say. . . . The villages also must have their visitors to inquire what lectures the bagpipe and the rebeck reads, even to the ballatry and the gamut of every municipal fiddler . . ." Milton wrote these words as a *reductio ad absurdum* in 1644. Three centuries later the absurdity came to pass in Soviet Russia, where the state has imposed its control even on composers as distinguished as Shostakovich and Prokofiev.

The Russian Communists and their apologists overseas have praised the USSR so loudly for its support of scientific

18 *Ibid.*
19 Julian Huxley, *Heredity, East and West* (New York, 1949), p. 163.

research that it comes somewhat as a surprise to find how far the Communist Party has gone since World War II in shackling natural science to the car of dialectical material-ism. As early as 1909 Lenin published a book entitled *Materialism and Empirio-Criticism* in the belief that the future of communism was threatened by false doctrines concern-ing the validity and meaning of scientific principles in the field of physics.[20] In 1938 the Astronomical Section of the Soviet Academy of Sciences branded the concept of rela-tivity as counter-revolutionary. Since World War II, the conflict between Soviet ideology and freedom in the natural sciences has become intensified. The idea of a finite but ex-panding universe, which many Western astronomers regard as a consequence of relativity, came under the ban of the Academy of Sciences in 1949. One of the speakers referred to relativity as a "cancerous tumor that gnaws through modern astronomical theory and is the main ideological enemy of materialist astronomy." The Communist Party has also at-tacked the application of probability theory, in the form of mathematical statistics, both to the various branches of sci-ence, especially biology, and to practical affairs.[21]

The most far-reaching illustration of the subjection of Soviet scientists to the concepts of dialectical materialism is the official ban on the whole science of genetics, as de-veloped in the Western world by Mendel, Morgan, and their successors. We are better posted on this development than on some other phases of Soviet violations of freedom in education, because Professor H. J. Muller, foremost of American geneticists and laureate of the Nobel Institute, spent four years at the Institute of Genetics in Moscow from

[20] James B. Conant, *Science and Common Sense* (New Haven, 1951), p. 349.
[21] Huxley, *Heredity, East and West*, pp. 171n, 193n.

1933 to 1937 and, like several British writers on this great Russian controversy, came to know many of the participants. The most distinguished of these, N. I. Vavilov, suffered the loss of his scientific posts, exile to Siberia, and death.

The nature of this controversy, which George Bernard Shaw did something to obfuscate, has been made clear by Julian Huxley in his book, *Heredity East and West.*[22] It is relatively unimportant that the Russians have sought to exalt the old plant-breeder, Michurin, who had some of the good qualities of Luther Burbank and like him wrote a deal of nonsense about genetic theory. It is more interesting to know that Trofim Lysenko, a peasant-turned-plant-breeder whom Stalin has showered with honors and made a Hero of the Soviet Union, uses experimental techniques which fail to include the common safeguards observed by all Western geneticists, even those drilled into our third-year students in biology. Muller describes Lysenko's writings along theoretical lines as "the merest drivel."

But the real significance of the proscription of genetics in the USSR is the demonstration that when a branch of science is deemed by the Communist leaders to yield results which clash with the principles of dialectic materialism, then that science goes by the board. The USSR, like the State of Tennessee in the Scopes trial, felt convinced of its rightness and was ready to punish. Many of the Russian political and ideological leaders, according to Huxley, "seem to have wanted a theory of biological and human heredity which assigned the chief role in evolution to environment, and to

[22] See also H. J. Muller, "The Destruction of Science in the USSR," *Saturday Review of Literature*, December 4, 1948; "Back to Barbarism—Scientifically," *ibid.*, December 11, 1948; "It Still Isn't a Science," *ibid.*, April 16, 1949; and *Bulletin of the Atomic Scientists*, vol. 5, pp. 130-56, May 1949.

have disliked the idea, which was implicit in neo-Mendelism, of large innate differences necessarily existing between individuals."[23]

As Professor Muller points out, "it has taken thousands of years to build the basis of that freedom of inquiry and criticism which science requires. It has been possible only through the growth of democratic practices, and through the associated progress in physical techniques, in living standards, and in education, applied on a grand scale. Only in modern times have all these conditions advanced sufficiently to permit that widespread, organized, objective search for truth which we think of when we use the word science."[24] Now Russia turns the clock back.

Most significant of all is the readiness with which the Russian geneticists surrendered their convictions once they had learned that Lysenko had the backing of the Central Committee of the party. They had to choose between setting science above their party or their party above science. They chose the latter, though one of them had the grace, in his speech of renunciation, to say that it would be "an extremely difficult and painful process."[25]

As Huxley says,

The issue could not be stated more clearly. Do we want science to continue as the free pursuit of knowledge of and control over nature, or do we want it to become subordinate to political theory and the slave of national governments?[26]

✿   ✿   ✿

To my way of thinking, Russia's destruction of freedom

[23] *Heredity East and West*, p. 25.
[24] *Saturday Review of Literature*, April 16, 1949, p. 61.
[25] T. M. Sonneborn, "Heredity, Environment and Politics," *Science*, vol. cxi, May, 1950, p. 539.
[26] *Heredity East and West*, p. 234.

in education holds a twofold lesson for us in America. First, we cannot permit the state to define truth for American scholars. And second, we cannot permit Americans who accept the Communist doctrine that party interests come ahead of scientific truth to hold membership in the goodly company of scholars.

During the First World War, Sir Arthur Quiller-Couch, Professor of English Literature at Cambridge University, became sorely troubled lest Britain, locked in a death grapple with Germany, take on too many of the traits of her enemy. He published a novel entitled *Foe-Farrell,* in which the two protagonists, each steeped in hatred of the other, grow to resemble each other so closely that at the end it becomes hard to tell one from the other. On the title page he placed the quotation: "The best revenge on your enemy is not to be like him." We should remember that slogan whenever a proposal comes up for state control of science, the humanities or the arts. And we of the academic world should remember it when defining the criteria necessary for membership in the company of scholars.

Ignazio Silone, in his account of the reasons that led him to quit the Communist Party, tells of a meeting of a special commission of the Executive of the Communist International, at which the topic of discussion was an ultimatum issued by the central committee of the British trade unions, ordering its local branches not to support the Communist-led minority movement, on pain of expulsion. The Russian delegate, Piatnisky, said that the solution was obvious. "The branches," he suggested, "should declare that they submit to the discipline demanded, and then, in practice, should do exactly the contrary." "But that would be a lie," interrupted the British Communist delegate. "Loud laughter," says

Silone, "greeted this ingenuous objection. Frank, cordial, interminable laughter, the like of which the gloomy offices of the Communist International had perhaps never heard before."[27]

Are men who laugh at truth or sacrifice their reason to the dictates of party to be deemed fit members of the company of scholars? An Old Testament passage comes to my mind: "And Joram said unto Jehu, is it peace, Jehu? And Jehu answered, what hast thou to do with peace?"

[27] Richard Crossman, ed., *The God That Failed* (New York, 1949), pp. 103-4.